Drugs
for Young People:
Their Use and
Misuse

Second (revised) Edition

by
KENNETH LEECH
and
BRENDA JORDAN

D1202828

THE RELIGIOUS EDUCATION PRESS
(A member of the Pergamon Group)

HEADINGTON HILL HALL   OXFORD

Distributed in the United States and Canada exclusively by Pergamon Press, Inc., Fairview Park, Elmsford, New York 10523.

Pergamon Press Ltd, Headington Hill Hall, Oxford, OX3 0BW

Pergamon Press Inc., Maxwell House, Fairview Park, Elmsford, New York 10523

Pergamon of Canada Ltd, 207 Queen's Quay West, Toronto 1

Pergamon Press (Aust.) Pty Ltd, 19a Boundary Street, Rushcutters Bay, N.S.W. 2011, Australia

Copyright © 1973

Kenneth Leech and Brenda Jordan

Library of Congress Catalog Card No. 67–31029

Second edition 1974

Printed in Great Britain by A. Wheaton & Co., Exeter.

ISBN 0 08 017938 X

CONTENTS

ABOUT THE AUTHORS

KENNETH LEECH and BRENDA JORDAN have been intimately involved in depth with the problem of drugs and drug addiction in both the practical and theoretical fields. Kenneth Leech was for four years a priest in Soho and has done much to counsel and befriend those suffering from drug addiction. Brenda Jordan, a psychologist and an expert on delinquency and mental illness, has worked in this sphere over a long period. They both write with sympathy and understanding as well as with expert knowledge.

INTRODUCTION

In this book we have tried to discuss openly and as factually as possible the problems of the *misuse* of drugs. We do not intend to moralise or to preach about the 'evils' of drug-taking; nor are we concerned here to decide whether drug-taking is wrong. The book is not propaganda against drugs. What we have tried to do is to outline the pros and the cons, to set out the facts, including the dangers, of drug misuse, so that you can make your own decisions, responsibly.

We have tried to avoid using unnecessary technical jargon. But, since drugs are chemicals, we cannot avoid using some technical terms: these we have explained. Some of the chapters are heavy going, but this is, after all, a difficult subject.

NOTE TO TEACHERS

It is hoped that the book will be found useful in current affairs lessons. Each chapter ends with questions for discussion, and there is a detailed bibliography containing both popular and more detailed studies on the question of drug misuse.

ACKNOWLEDGEMENTS

We wish to thank all our junkie friends and all friends whether drug takers, doctors, psychiatrists, psychologists, hippies, etc. who have given us the first-hand information for our research, and who have patiently criticised the manuscript. In particular, we would like to thank Jill Horwitz, the late Peter Jewell, Alan Newman, Lenny Payne, Keith Vinall, Gloria Wilkinson and Geoffrey Worthington: also Dorothy Coutts, formerly of the London School of Economics, Mr. H. B. Spear of the Home Office Drugs Branch, and Dr. J. H. Willis of King's College Hospital Addiction Unit, who gave valuable information and references.

1

WHAT ARE DRUGS?

IF you have been a patient in hospital you have probably been very pleased to receive your medicines when the nurse brought round the drug trolley. You will also have seen how careful they are always to keep the drug trolleys locked or attended by a nurse when open. Every drug that you have is checked by two qualified people, to make sure it is the right one and that the action of one drug does not interfere with that of another. Before any new drug is given, a doctor must be consulted, who then writes a prescription, even in the case of sleeping draughts, laxatives and headache pills. Each medicine prescribed is then checked by two trained staff to ensure that the right amount of the right drug is being administered to the patient.

What are drugs anyway? A drug is a chemical which affects us mentally or physically. In the normal way, drugs are only used for medical purposes and are the chemical ingredients which go to make up a doctor's prescription. The science of actually making up the drugs is called *pharmacy*. Often a chemist shop will have a sign outside saying 'pharmacist', showing that qualified persons are employed to make up doctors' prescriptions. Research pharmacologists are making many of today's big medical advances, turning dangerous viruses into docile vaccines, extracting powerful germ-killing agents, such as the penicillin group, from fungi and bacteria and by synthetic means. There are synthetic hormones and vitamins for those who lack them; powders and pills to beat malaria and tuberculosis; drugs to treat allergies, diabetes, some mental disorders, leprosy, high blood pressure, etc.

Even antiseptics, disinfectants and insecticides are drugs, and are used to destroy or inhibit the growth of micro-organisms in the patient's environment and on the body surface. Dettol, for instance, is a multi-purpose antiseptic used for cleaning wounds, etc., and not only kills germs but stays active to inhibit their further growth. A soothing ointment to put on cuts and grazes is medicinal zinc and castor oil (or similar preparations) which stops many a small child's tears as it takes away the stinging pain.

The *vaccines* are used mainly to produce an active immunity to a variety of *diseases:* an immunity which may vary in duration from months to years, or even a lifetime. Those vaccines used most often are for smallpox, tuberculosis, typhoid, typhus and yellow fever. The vaccines themselves are killed or *attenuated* forms of the bacteria causing the illness. Immunization is for prevention for life, and the *serum* (the substance used) is derived from the blood of animals that have been immunized against the toxin secreted by the organisms.

Another group of drugs enables the doctor to diagnose or find out what is wrong with the patient, A simple solution containing specific colours is frequently used to show up 'scratches' on a damaged cornea; other drugs are used to detect stomach ulcers, liver disorders and kidney functioning. Often the drug prepares the organ so that it shows up clearly under X-ray.

Luckily for us, the list is very long, and drugs can be found to treat and cure nearly all the diseases we are victims to. Of course, we still need to find cures for many illnesses which ravage our lives, such as cancer, some forms of arthritis and poliomyelitis. Where no cure has yet been discovered we can at least alleviate some of the suffering.

In fact, we have even become very adept at treating ourselves. For example, if we feel sick after too much rich food, or if we have a headache or a cough, we do not go to the doctor, but take one of the easily available preparations we can buy without prescription. It is quite usual for families to have a 'medicine cabinet' where drugs such as aspirin, cough-mixture, laxatives, travel pills, etc. are kept for everyday use. We have grown up in an atmosphere where, if we feel ill, we immediately take something for it and expect to be cured. Only if we consider it 'serious' do we bother to go to the doctor or hospital. Instead of waiting for a long time in the surgery we find it quicker to get something at the chemist's.

Drug use and misuse

In these circumstances certain drugs have become used wrongly, or are misused. For example, if we have a headache or toothache for a week and keep on taking more and more pills for relieving the pain, we are misusing both the drug and ourselves. Any ache or pain is meant to serve as a warning that the system is not functioning properly or is 'breaking down'. The toothache is probably telling us that something is quite wrong and we should go to the dentist for a filling, or have the tooth out. We could have both a headache and a toothache and continue taking, say, aspirin, and suddenly find we have an abscess in one tooth. The headache and toothache are only *symptoms* of the real trouble. If we are always wide awake, 'edgy', nervous and can't sleep, we should not automatically take sleeping-pills or tranquillizers. We should attend to what may appear unimportant, but are often vital, details, such as room ventilation, extraneous noises, too many pillows, too few clothes. If all these things do not help it is *then* time to ask the doctor's advice. Likewise, if we are always feeling tired and worn out, once we have eliminated the obvious, such as not sufficient sleep, we should consult the doctor. Tiredness is often the warning signal of a more serious disorder.

Let us look at some of the uses drugs have been put to in the treating of diseases:

For LEPROSY – SULPHETRONE

This drug is one of the sulphate compounds which arrests the progress of certain forms of leprosy although it may take five years to do so. The agony of leprosy has to be seen to be believed, and the mental anguish of a person who first realizes he has leprosy can now be abated by the knowledge that treatment is available, and that his limbs will not just turn into useless sore lumps and stubs, as those of his leprous forefathers did.

For MALARIA – CAMOQUIN and PRIMAQUINE

This is one of the anti-malarial drugs. One ingredient kills the malaria parasites in the blood plasma; another kills the parasite inside the red blood cells. Large numbers of people used to die from malaria each year; camoprima is now used to prevènt people contracting malaria, and its use, were it more widely available in countries where malaria is endemic, could save many thousands of lives.

For EPILEPSY – MYSOLINE (with phenytoin)

This drug incorporates two anti-convulsants that reduce either in number, or degree of severity, epileptic fits. They are 'depressants' which affect the central nervous system, inhibiting the sudden discharge of motor energy, which is the phrase used to describe epileptic fits. Drugs like this allow people suffering from this inhibiting ailment to lead a relatively normal life.

For TUBERCULOSIS (T.B.) – PYCAMISAN

This contains substances which are conquering tuberculosis, the scourge of the 19th Century in Britain and other industrialized countries. The disease still rages in countries which are not so fortunate and advanced regarding health matters as Britain. Care for the old and poor, free chest X-rays for all, are available in Britain and help to prevent the disease getting 'set in' unnoticed.

TO STOP INFECTIONS – PENICILLIN

Everyone knows about the antibiotic penicillin which was discovered by Sir Alexander Fleming in a manner so often characteristic of great scientific discoveries and inventions. Although Fleming discovered the drug in St. Mary's Hospital, Paddington, London, in 1929, it only came into general use about 1944–45. For years, mouldy bread had been used as a home remedy for infections, and today most antibiotics are derived originally from moulds or bacteria. Penicillin is available in an endless number of preparations, and new ones are marketed very frequently. It is made in a number of types (F. G. K. O. V. X.), but type G is the one most commonly used. Penicillin is an antibiotic and helps to stop many infections raging in the sick patient, while preventing infections spreading. It also brings down high temperature.

For CURING ALCOHOLISM – DISULFIRAM (Alcophobin, Antabuse)

This drug is used to discourage the intake of alcohol in people who drink an excessive amount – too much to be able to stop (alcoholics). It enables supportive treatment and psychotherapy to be given. (Psychotherapy is a form of psychiatric help and is concerned with healing the disturbed personality). The drug used alone has no effect, but in the presence of alcohol, it produces such distressing symptoms – nausea, vomiting, palpitations – that the patient becomes very ill and distressed and does not wish them to recur. After a few such experiences he, in all probability, refuses to imbibe alcohol any more, particularly if he continues to take the drug.

Other drugs however, although they have legitimate medical uses, have become misused, that is self-administered, without instructions from a doctor.

PEP PILLS (see also chapter 3) are very much misused. Many people who can't keep up with their work, their problems, their families, etc. either have been given pep pills by their doctor, or have obtained them by other means (that is, illicitly). Many millions of these pills are prescribed annually by doctors and many people continue taking them all the time instead of just very occasionally. Dexedrine ('dexies'), for example, is a pep pill of the *amphetamine* group (the pharmacological group name). It is a mental stimulant which can combat post-illness inertia and some forms of depression when used clinic· ally. One of its effects is to suppress the appetite and it is, therefore, widely prescribed by doctors for reducing the weight of people who are too fat to be healthy. Other effects of this drug have been found by some people to make them feel 'more cheerful', 'able to concentrate', etc., and they foolishly take the drug without a doctor's advice. They are foolish because they have not taken the trouble to find out why they need an artificial way of being cheerful, or why they can't concentrate, or why they feel tired; they may be suffering from some form of diabetes for which they should be receiving treatment.

Another drug of this group which is misused is *Drinamyl* ('blues'), formerly referred to as 'purple hearts'. This drug is prescribed to alleviate anxiety without causing drowsiness in patients. It is, in fact, a compound of amphetamine (for stimulation) and barbiturate (for sedation).

The amphetamines affect the central nervous system, and stimulate the cerebral cortex of the brain. They also cause insomnia (not being able to sleep), restlessness and an artificial sense of well-being or *euphoria*. After an oral dose (by mouth) the individual is more alert and better able to work. After a large dose, physical exertion may be much increased, but when it has worn off, there is a greater fatigue and depression than before, and a longer period of rest is required. In misuse situations, the misuser keeps taking more of the drug in an endeavour to avoid this 'coming down' feeling of greater fatigue and greater depression. This then causes overstimulation – a form of making the body and the brain work at greater speed for unnatural and prolonged periods. In some cases it can cause heart failure, increased blood-pressure, disorientation and hallucinations.

An amphetamine which has been used irresponsibly is *Methedrine* (methylamphetamine hydrochloride). Methedrine is used clinically for treating some brain illness and is used in chronic fatigue states, mild depressions, chronic headaches of psychogenic (that is, not organic) origin, and also to control excessive overweight in some instances. The 'side effects' (adverse reactions from the drug produced in some patients) and dangers are the same as for any drugs of the amphetamine group mentioned above.

A drug of similar action is *Preludin* (phenmetrazine): while not as strong as an amphetamine, it has similar side effects. It is mainly used as a slimming pill and euphoriant when medically prescribed, and the main danger of self-medication is that it can induce a very severe mental disturbance.

THE BARBITURATES (see also chapter 3) are medically prescribed for sedation, to reduce tension in migraine headache sufferers, etc. and, in various forms, are widely used for many purposes. They are often used with the amphetamines and also affect the central nervous system.

Some of the most usual drugs of this type are *pheno-*

barbitone, Nembutal, Sodium Amytal and Soneryl (capital letters signify Trade names). These drugs are most effective in slowing down the activities of the brain to a level of non-excitement and, in many preparations, to help people sleep who can't do so normally (in the form of sleeping pills). It is sometimes necessary for people who, for example, have had brain operations, to continue using these drugs every day, under medical supervision. One such drug is phenobarbitone, which can be given over a long period of time.

It is most important to remember that when any of these drugs are being used the patient must keep them away from the bedside, as it is known that upon waking, confusion often exists. The person may wake up and forget which pills they are and take more for headache, stomach ache, etc.

Although the barbiturates work by depressing the central nervous system, certain preparations affect, mainly, the motor centres in the brain. These tranquillizing drugs make the individual feel calm when taken in the right doses. When taken in too great a quantity they may cause delayed reflex action to occur. It is thus dangerous to do such things as driving a car or operating machinery, because we respond to things more slowly than we normally do after taking these drugs.

Heavy doses cause respiratory and cardiac depression and are very dangerous (for example, an overdose of barbiturates can cause death). Most of the barbiturates tend to lower the blood pressure.

Adverse reactions likely when the drugs are misused are acute mental confusion, drowsiness, rapid pulse, alleviation in blood pressure, skin irritation, collapse and even coma. It is highly dangerous to consume alcohol when under the influence of barbiturates. In some cases misuse of the barbiturates can cause amnesia (loss of memory) anaemia and renal (kidney) damage. Often such diseases can occur without the knowledge of the taker, and grave damage is done to his body and brain.

THE NARCOTICS (see also chapter 4). The most important drugs of this group are *opium* and its derivatives. Included in the group are the opium powders and ipecac, paregoric and synthetic preparations from (or similar to) opium: the *morphines*, *codeines* and diacetyl-morphine (called *heroin*). They are analgesics and used to relieve pain and induce sleep (especially when sleep is prevented by pain), and to check such things as coughing and diarrhoea when a person has had an operation. Morphine and codeine* affect the cerebral cortex mainly. Morphine is the marvellous drug which relieves intense pain, and codeine reduces coughing. Others in this group relax smooth muscle tissue (for example, muscles of the digestive system—not the muscles such as biceps).

It is not known exactly how these drugs work, but they affect the central nervous system and depress the cerebral cortex, and probably areas in the brain called the thalamus and the hypothalamus, which are most important in connection with regulating our emotions and our food and drink intake. Morphine and the opiates produce euphoria and relief from fear and apprehension, but slow down both mental and physical activity. It is a strong respiratory depressant, but only affects heart and blood-pressure to a minor degree. There is an increase in perspiration, relaxation of muscle tissue and a contraction of the pupils of the eyes.

The strange thing about the opiates, and the amphetamines and barbiturates to a lesser extent, is that they produce something called 'tolerance', or adaptation to use. This means that more and more of the drug is needed

*Not in the same concentration as sold in chemists' shops under the name 'codeine'.

in order to produce the same effect – pain-killing with morphine, for example. Apart from this most serious effect, the opiates can cause acute poisoning, dizziness, nausea, pin-point pupils, slow respiration, coma and even death in severe cases of overdose. Unfortunately, morphine can also have side effects, such as constipation, nausea, vomiting, and itching, which are not desirable in a patient who has just had an operation.

Heroin (which is the drug of this group mainly misused in Britain) resembles morphine, from which it is prepared by acetylation (a heating process used in pharmacology). It was first produced in 1898 and sold as a substitute for morphine and codeine. It was even promoted as a cure for those people who were addicted to morphine (that is, who found they could not live without the drug and needed greater and greater doses in order either to prevent their pain – in cases of cancer sufferers – or to maintain their feeling of being able to cope with life.) Heroin was used as a sedative in cough-mixture and to relieve intense pain very widely before it was realized that it is the most highly addictive of all the opium derivatives.

Cocaine comes from the South American coca shrub. It used to be used in dentistry because of the anaesthetic and euphoric effect it produced. Now other and safer local anaesthetics with less dangerous effects are used. Its action is on the peripheral nervous system (reflex actions for example), causing the nerve-endings to be rendered incapable of receiving and transmitting impulses (hence, its use when the dentist was filling a tooth!). Being a euphoriant as well as an anaesthetic it is widely used by some South American Indian tribes, like the Boro. These men chew for hours the paste formed by the coca powder while they are out hunting and working. Women, however, are forbidden to sample the drug!

When misused cocaine can produce anxiety, dizziness,

severe headache and convulsions; death sometimes occurs during misuse from cardio-vascular (heart) and respiratory failure.

THE HALLUCINOGENS (see also chapter 3)

LSD or Lysergic Acid Diethylamide is a drug of this group. The initials LSD are formed from its German name. The drug is used successfully by some psychiatrists in their clinical work. LSD acts on the central nervous system and may cause hallucinations. In this condition it is possible for the patient 'to go back in time' (regress) to a particular part of his life, usually childhood, and relive an event which happened then. This regression is often to an unpleasant or frightening event and can assist the psychiatrist in finding the patient's problems and thus can, perhaps, help in effecting a cure.

If it is taken without professional guidance and constant supervision, the person taking LSD may undergo a terrifying experience which has, perhaps, worried him unconsciously from childhood, and which he cannot sort out on his own. He then becomes very much worse and not able to cope with the distressing situation and may suffer a breakdown of personality, similar to some forms of schizophrenia. This is extremely dangerous if the person is without medical supervision, but more will be said about this in chapter 3.

Summing up

Drugs and modern medicine have revolutionized the life-span of man. So little time ago anyone having appendicitis would have died when the appendix burst. Death followed wounds which turned gangrenous. Blood transfusions today save many people's lives, but were unheard of a very few decades ago. In the field of tropical disease, scourges such as yaws, trachoma, leprosy, tape-worm, malaria, can now be brought under control, instead of taking their yearly toll of countless sufferings and lives.

Each one of us can look back and thank God for one drug or another which has either helped us ourselves or someone we love and may even have saved our lives. Some people are able today to continue living a normal life only because they are constantly being given drugs by their doctor. One can say that some people are in fact kept alive by drugs; for example, diabetic patients, who are unable to live without insulin. In the right medical hands drugs can, indeed, be wonderful instruments of healing.

QUESTIONS FOR DISCUSSION

1. What are drugs and what are they used for?
2. What is the difference between use and misuse of drugs?
3. Why should drugs not be misused? Give examples to illustrate your answer.
4. Discuss some of the advances in modern medicine and surgery made possible by the discovery of drugs.
5. What are amphetamines and what are they medically prescribed for?
6. Should doctors be prevented from prescribing barbiturates if people misuse them?
7. Why don't they stop manufacturing opiates and morphine if these drugs are dangerous?

2

BACKGROUND TO ADDICTION

IN the first chapter we introduced the use of drugs in a medical setting, outlined the various drugs which are commonly misused, and gave a brief pharmacological description of these drugs. This section will outline the nature of *addiction* to drugs. What does this mean, and what do all the other terms mean that are always occurring in reference to drug taking? *Addiction, Dependence, Habituation* and *Tolerance* – what do these terms mean?

It is popular to refer to drug-takers as being drug 'addicts'. This is inaccurate. There is a distinction between those who experiment with drugs for one reason or another and those who become dependent on them in everyday life. The latter category of persons can be termed 'addicted' to drugs.

A committee under the chairmanship of Lord Brain, set up by the British Government to advise on drugs liable to cause addiction, issued the following definition in its first report in 1961. (This definition was based on that in the World Health Organisation's seventh report, 1957):

> *Drug addiction* is a state of periodic or chronic intoxication produced by the repeated consumption of a drug (natural or synthetic); its characteristics include:
> 1. An overpowering desire or need (compulsion) to continue taking the drug and to obtain it by any means.
> 2. A tendency to increase the dose, though some patients may remain indefinitely on a stationary dose.
> 3. A psychological and physical dependence on the effects of the drug.

4. The appearance of a characteristic 'abstinence syndrome'*
in a subject from whom the drug is withdrawn.
5. An effect detrimental to the individual and to society.

In 1965 the same committee thought fit to define an
addict as 'a person who, as the result of repeated admini-
stration, has become dependent upon a drug controlled
under the Dangerous Drugs Act and has an overpowering
desire for its continuance, but who does not require it for
the relief of organic disease'. This definition covers addiction not only to heroin and cocaine, but to all the drugs
mentioned in the Dangerous Drugs Act**, which includes
morphine, pethidine, methadone and codeine.

Simply, this means that an addicted person is one who
is both physically and psychologically dependent on drugs,
usually of the narcotic type (heroin and morphine for
example) but also of the amphetamine and barbiturate
types. *Narcotic* means scientifically all the drugs used as
tranquilizers, sedatives and sleeping pills, but it is commonly used internationally to refer only to drugs like
opium, morphine, heroin, pethidine, cocaine, etc., which
are subject to measures of international control.

But we need to go deeper than this, and examine what
we mean by *dependence*. There are, then, two types of
dependence on drugs: there is the purely physical dependence and there is a psychological one. The former is
produced by the addictive drugs (see chapter 1), particularly the narcotics and barbiturates, and they are liable
to produce a physical *tolerance*. This is the condition
whereby after taking the drugs for some time the body
machinery, or *metabolism*, needs the drug in order to

* 'Abstinence syndrome' means the pattern of physical and mental
symptoms and behaviour which occurs when the patient/addict
'abstains' from, or does not have, the drug he is addicted to.
** The former Dangerous Drugs Acts were superseded by the
Misuse of Drugs Act 1971. More will be said about this in Chapter
Three.

function at what is a tolerable level to the user. The user is compelled to increase the doses of the drug, in most cases, in order to arrive at the desired effect, or to stave off *withdrawal symptoms*. At this stage absolute stoppage of the drug can cause severe and painful repercussions and in some cases death. The symptoms are very much the same in each patient and the whole process is called the 'withdrawal or abstinence syndrome'. The habitual use of large amounts of alcohol, barbiturates, and certain other drugs, as well as the narcotics, also produces physical dependence with withdrawal symptoms when these drugs are abruptly discontinued. However, the physical dependence created by alcohol and the barbiturates differs from that of the narcotics. Small doses of alcohol and barbiturates can be taken regularly over long periods without producing noticeable physical dependence. The sustained use of even small doses of the narcotics always leads to physical dependence. Although cocaine produces no troublesome physical dependence, it is the most harmful to health in the opinion of many experts! Users of large doses become so anxious and prone to delusions that they often imagine they are in grave danger and must protect themselves from imaginary enemies (this type of mental illness is called *paranoid schizophrenia*).

The psychological dependence (or emotional dependence) on drugs refers to the psychological meaning which the addicted person places upon the use of the drugs and their effects. This is often referred to as *habituation*, or the habitual use of drugs. The Brain Committee in 1961, again following the W.H.O., defined drug habituation as 'a condition resulting from the repeated consumption of a drug. Its characteristics include:

1. A desire (but not compulsion) to continue taking the drug for the sense of improved well-being which it engenders.
2. Little or no tendency to increase the dose.

3. Some degree of psychological dependence on the effect of the drug, but absence of physical dependence and hence of an abstinence syndrome.

4. Detrimental effects, if any, primarily on the individual.'

This means that the user has produced a *habit* of using the drug. This definition tried to define types of drug use which were supposed not to produce physical dependence. But the amphetamines and barbiturates to which it was directed have sometimes very dangerous psychological dependence together with a physical dependence. Dr. P. H. Connell of the Maudsley Hospital has described the amphetamines as being capable of bringing about a state of mind which is clinically (or to a psychiatrist) indistinguishable from paranoid schizophrenia. This, being a very serious mental disease, takes a long time to cure. People who have suffered from these effects of the amphetamines or 'pep pills' describe the state as 'the horrors', and it is a temporary condition characterized by terrifying hallucinations of persecution and pursuit (as mentioned above in connection with cocaine).

The psychological dependence on drugs is much harder to define and perhaps it is easier to illustrate with analogies. One does not physically need to drink tea or coffee (although they are both stimulants) or to watch television, but the person can become so used to the habit that he feels he cannot live without it' Often drugs cause a change of mood or 'personality' and, although there is no medical reason for taking the drug, the user feels that drugs offer means of escaping from some problem, such as relief from tiredness, worry or strain.

The trouble here is that the root cause of the problem is put aside and not sorted out and dealt with. If you are continually tired and take pep pills to overcome it, you may very well be doing yourself untold harm. There is usually a good reason why you are tired and it is the body's way of telling you to 'ease up – you are working me too fast – I can't cope', and you may very well find yourself in hospital for a long time.

No person leading a full and stimulating life, who is not mentally or physically ill really needs to take drugs. When such a healthy person takes drugs and becomes dependent on them in order to effect a change of personality or mood, there is something wrong which needs professional attention. If drugs are used to escape from boredom, then it is only a temporary relief and it is much better to find out why you are bored instead of becoming dependent on pills, so that you are utterly miserable when you have none.

For the purposes of this book we can, therefore, define addiction to drugs as being 'the state where there is a physical or biological need, together, probably, with a psychological dependence on it'; and dependence as being 'the state where there is no known physical dependence. but a definite psychological one'. *This is the difference between addiction and dependence.*

More about addiction

With heroin addiction, putting aside the actual physical dependence caused by the drug itself, there is a psychological dependence. This has been illustrated in one case known to the authors, by substituting water for heroin, which was injected by the addict into himself in the usual way. (The addict, of course, did not know that it was only water.) It was discovered that the effects were the same as if he had actually taken the real drug. This is an example of the psychological dependence on the drug – the power of the drug and its associations of well-being and sheer relief from anxiety had in fact *conditioned* the addict. 'Conditioning' is a psychological term and takes place when, for example, during experiments over a period of time, a bell follows an electric shock applied to an animal's leg (see the work of the Russian physiologist, Pavlov). The shock causes a reflex withdrawal of the leg. After a number of pairings of the bell and shock in this way the leg flexion response can be elicited by the sound of the bell *only*. The animal is said to be 'conditioned' to produce this response by the association of the bell and the shock.

Another common form of conditioning which produces psychological dependence is that illustrated by the seemingly compulsive use of 'fruit machines' and other forms of gambling by some people, where an occasional reward will keep them happily employed at this entertainment for hours. In the laboratory a pigeon can be made to peck at a bar for hours in the hopes that he will get an occasional reward of a grain. An American psychologist called Skinner (1957) got pigeons to produce 6,000 pecks an hour for the reward of just 12 single grains!

Most people who become compulsively drawn to continue their habit or hobby wrongly think that they will be able to stop it whenever they want, even if experience shows that other people in the same plight cannot stop. You have seen this occur with cigarette smokers, beer drinkers, television serial followers and gamblers, no doubt. Alcohol is sought by some people as solace in their troubles. Although this particular habit may start as a psychological one, it can develop into a physical one, when the person finds he is an alcoholic, and physically needs a certain amount of ethyl alcohol in his blood stream every day.

Cannabis (variously called marijuana, hashish, 'pot', 'tea', 'weed', etc. See chapter 3) is smoked in preference to drinking alcohol in many countries, either because it is cheaper, or because it has mystical or even religious associations. In Muslim countries, for example, no alcohol is drunk as it is forbidden by Muslim law, but in many of these countries cannabis is smoked in much the same way as whisky is drunk in this country.

With all these habits the problem is how to control their effect on everyday living, so that you are in control of the habit, not the habit in control of you. Very often a patient addicted to heroin and cocaine will tell you he thought he could 'manage his habit' in the beginning and that although he saw others get 'hooked' (addicted) he would not become so himself, because he thought he could always stop taking the drug when he wanted to.

The unfortunate thing about addiction is that unconsciously the addict in this position knows that his use of the drug is for psychological dependence only (for he feels he can give it up when he wants), and at the beginning feels no physical need to continue taking it, but he does not realise that the tolerance rate is increasing. It is a pity, but it seems that a potential addict just begins to realise the statement is true that he *can* become physically dependent on the drug just at the same time that he *is* physically dependent on it. The state which is then arrived at is called, in addicts' terminology, being 'hooked' – like a fish at the end of an angler's line!

Therapeutic addiction

We cannot leave the subject of addiction without reference to those people who have become addicted to drugs through their legitimate use during medical treatment. Many thousands of people in this country are dependent upon barbiturates in order to sleep, or in order to keep their anxieties down to a manageable level, and these drugs are prescribed by their doctors. Others need stimulation at certain times, or are prescribed amphetamines by doctors in connection with slimming for medical purposes. Some persons are in such pain, for example in the latter stages of cancer, that they are prescribed narcotics, and, in the course of their treatment, become addicted to them. It is important here to quote a few figures, to show how, before drugs were being misused by a large number of people ignorant or casual about their effects, persons had become addicted through their use in certain medical circumstances. These are called therapeutic addicts.

NUMBERS OF THERAPEUTIC ADDICTS IN GREAT BRITAIN

1962	1963	1964	1965	1966	1967	1968	1969	1970	1971
312	355	368	344	351	313	306	289	295	265

The 1961 Brain Report quoted examples of such therapeutic addicts and to elucidate this point one such case is given below:

> Mrs. E. is a manic-depressive [that is, she was suffering from a severe mental illness known by that name] of middle age. Her persistent symptom is low back pain for which she has had operations. In addition she . . . has been an in-patient in a mental hospital. Her record includes reports from very many consultants. Nine years ago she was treated with pethidine [a narcotic drug]. A year-and-a-half later this was changed to methadone [another narcotic drug], the dose of 10 mg. every six hours having remained unchanged all this time. On this quantity she does all her own housework. In her better phases she has voluntarily reduced the dosage temporarily to some extent. When, however, the drug was withdrawn altogether, during the time that she was an in-patient at the mental hospital, a profound nervous disturbance immediately followed.

Unlike most people who become heroin addicts (for example) in most of these therapeutics cases the addict *is* able to withstand the need for increased dosage and remains constant at a certain level of tolerance. It must be remembered, however, that the patient is under the care and scrutiny of a doctor, and other drugs may be used in connection with the therapeutic dosage of the addictive drug, which enables the patient to become stabilised on a particular dosage, but continue to be dependent on it even when the original necessity for the use has disappeared.

Naturally, drugs known to be addictive are given only with the utmost care and consideration by doctors, and their use is limited to extreme cases and for short lengths of time – for example, to relieve pain for 2–3 days immediately following an operation.

If some drugs are addictive why use them?

Why indeed? We saw in chapter 1 the medical use of addictive drugs, and more will be said about the needs of the person who finds he must use such drugs in chapter 5. However, many people 'experiment' with drugs without knowing the dangers involved. In some cases drugs have been tried because 'others do it', and it is felt to be the 'in thing', the craze which everyone is following – or say they are. You often find, on careful questioning, that not only do these people often not take drugs themselves, but they are completely ignorant of

(a) what the drugs are supposed to do,
(b) what the safe dose is,
(c) which drugs are supposed to do what,
(d) how you are supposed to take them,
(e) what their effects will be over a long term.

We are left with a silly situation where the person wishes to be 'different', but in fact follows blindly other people taking part in the craze. The difference is that unlike other crazes this one is dangerous because in its final form either it can be lethal (taking heroin and cocaine for example) or its effects can be felt for many years because it is not easy to stop being addicted – and it takes a great deal of time, energy and work.

In the next chapter we shall discuss how the misuse of certain drugs has become a problem in Britain.

QUESTIONS FOR DISCUSSION

1. Explain the differences between 'addiction' and 'dependence' when talking about drugs.
2. What is psychological dependence on a drug?
3. Why has it not been recommended that drugs should be withdrawn immediately when an addicted person has, for example, been committed to a hospital?
4. Is there any justification in 'just trying' the highly addictive drugs like heroin or morphine?
5. Do you think it would be wise to stop the use of all drugs known to be addictive? If not, why not?
6. Why has LSD not been discussed in this chapter?

3

THE DRUG PROBLEM IN BRITAIN

THE 'SOFT' DRUGS

'The Drug Problem'

WE read a lot in the newspapers about 'the drug problem'. Much of it is exaggerated and distorted. Newspaper men cannot always distinguish between different types of drugs, and one has, therefore, to treat articles on drugs with very great caution.

There are several 'drug problems' in Britain. The use of large quantities of tranquillizers, sedatives, sleeping tablets, pills of all kinds, raises problems. The use of 'pep pills' by teenagers ignorant of their effects is a problem. A problem numerically less serious, but more serious in terms of the effect on the personality, is the spread of addiction to so-called 'hard drugs' – heroin and similar agents. The 'problems' in the use of these drugs are constituted by the harmful, and sometimes fatal, effects which the drugs may have on the individual and on society. In this chapter, more detailed accounts are given of the main types of 'soft drugs' which are misused in this country, some of which were briefly described in chapter 1.

Socially Acceptable Drugs

But, before we go on to describe these 'drugs of misuse', we need to remind ourselves that the two most commonly misused drugs are both socially acceptable, and we do not therefore think of them as part of the 'drug problem' at all. They are tobacco and alcohol. This book is not primarily concerned with them, but we ought not to continue this chapter without at least mentioning them and their effects.

Tobacco is a mental stimulant which excites the brain but without altering consciousness. It is derived from three types of nicotine weed – *nicotiana tabacum*, *nicotiana rustica*, and *nicotiana latissima*. Nicotine is the *active principle* in tobacco; if you remove the nicotine content, there is little point or pleasure in smoking. When a cigarette is smoked, the mouth is filled with a mixture of carbon particles and a variety of invisible substances, including carbon monoxide.

Sometimes an inexperienced smoker will suffer painful effects because some centres of the brain are stimulated and so the blood pressure falls, the pulse slows down, and there may follow sweating and sickness. But once the tobacco *habit* has developed, the blood pressure rises and *adrenalin* is released. But with *excessive* smoking, there may be such effects as chronic laryngitis, palpitations of the heart, and shortage of breath. The most important effects of nicotine are on both the autonomic nervous system and the brain. This is why, if a man is over excited, he can be soothed by tobacco, or if he is depressed a smoke may help. But there may be very dangerous side effects, the most obvious being lung cancer.

Alcohol, the other major 'respectable' drug, can have very serious effects when taken in excessive quantities. Continual heavy drinking can lead to bodily changes and to illnesses, physical and mental. The alcoholic suffers from malnutrition, liver diseases, and inflammation of the stomach. He may also go through the mental effects of loss of memory, decline in intelligence and hallucinations.

Alcohol is produced from the fermentation by yeast of sugars from plants (such as beer from barley, wine from grapes, and cider from apples) and the concentration of alcohol is increased by distilling. This is how we get spirits

– gin, whisky, rum, etc. When it is drunk, alcohol acts upon the nervous system as a *depressant*. But one of the first of the functions which it depresses is the power of restraint, and this is why, after drinking alcohol, we lose our inhibitions; we become less shy, more talkative, etc. Thus people have come to think that alcohol is a stimulant, whereas its effect is to reduce nervous activity, so that after continual heavy drinking there are acute withdrawal symptoms.

Alcoholism is a killer disease and affects far more people in this country than do the drugs we are about to describe. There are around half a million alcoholics – those who are physically dependent on alcohol – in this country, and very many more who are to some degree dependent. Just because it is accepted in our society, we tend to forget how harmful the misuse of alcohol can be. If we remember this, it will help us to have a sense of proportion about the misused drugs with which we are concerned in this book.

The main Drugs of Misuse

Broadly speaking, there are five sets of drugs which are misused and the use of which either forms, or affects social problems in Britain.

First, there are the pills of *amphetamine* type, stimulants used for pep effects and therefore called 'pep pills'. These include *Benzedrine*, *Dexedrine*, *Methedrine* and *Preludin*. But the best-known pill is an amphetamine-barbiturate called *Drinamyl*, formerly known as the 'purple-heart'.

Secondly, there are the *barbiturates* and other sedatives, sleeping pills used to calm mind and body, and having therefore the opposite effect to that of the stimulants.

Thirdly, there is *cannabis*, marijuana or hashish, which is smoked in 'joints' or 'reefers' and which circulates widely throughout the country

Fourthly, there are the psychedelic, or 'mind-expanding' drugs such as *LSD, psilocybin* and *mescalin.* The users of these drugs include intelligent people as well as many who use them simply for 'kicks'.

Fifthly, there are the 'hard' drugs like *heroin, morphine, methadone*, etc. Heroin is extremely dangerous: continually injected into the blood-stream, it can lead to a disintegration of body and mind and to premature death.

Until 1971 there were a number of different Acts controlling these various drugs, but they were consolidated by the Misuse of Drugs Act 1971. Under the Act, there are three classes of drugs, A, B and C. Class A includes opium, heroin, morphine, and most of the opiates, pethidine, LSD and other 'psychedelics'. Class B includes cannabis (except the pure material of the drug which is in Class A), and the amphetamines. Class C includes methaqualone (Mandrax) and others. The barbiturates remain outside these controls and are governed by the Poisons regulations.

Prescription forgery seems particularly common among women aged between 30 and 50, and the most popular forgeries are for amphetamines used for slimming purposes. In 1965 there were 460 cases of attempted forgery reported, and 349 people tried to pass 889 forged prescriptions. In 1965, 33 doctors reported the loss or theft of over 2,500 E.C.10 prescription forms, and in one case, 1,400 were stolen at once.

'Pep Pills'

What we call 'pep pills' belong to the amphetamine group. These drugs first began to be developed as long ago as 1887 but it was not until 1927 that amphetamine sulphate (Benzedrine) was first synthesised in the United States. In 1932 Smith, Kline and French produced the 'Benzedrine Inhaler'. Benzedrine was first used clinically in the United States in 1935 for treating *narcolepsy* (an illness where the patient has an uncontrollable inclination for sleep), and it was found that the drug brought relief from sleeping attacks. During the second world war, Benzedrine was widely used by the forces, as it had been used earlier in the Spanish Civil War, under the name of 'energy tablets'. Since then amphetamine drugs have become very popular, and have been used for the treatment of overweight, fatigue and depression, narcolepsy, alcoholism, barbiturate addiction, and bed-wetting. They have been used to treat forms of mental illness.*

There are today many varieties of amphetamine drugs. Most of those which circulate in Britain are legally manufactured, whereas in the U.S.A. they are made illicitly. Here amphetamines come in tablet or capsule form. Each drug has a particular size, shape and colour. But it is not possible to identify a tablet or capsule simply by looking at it, since there are very many different drugs which look almost exactly alike. To tell what a particular tablet is you need to analyse it. It is from their colour and shape that the amphetamine drugs have become known by nicknames. Thus the best-known drug is *Drinamyl*, a form of Dexedrine (dexamphetamine sulphate) combined with a barbiturate (amylobarbitone) to counter-act the 'pep' effect. Drinamyl, manufactured by Smith, Kline and French, became known as 'purple heart' because of its shape and colour. In 1964 the Pharmaceutical Society urged that the colour and shape be changed, and today

* You may see these drugs referred to either by their medical group or by their *trade* name. The group name, which is a much shorter form of the full *chemical* name, tells you what kind of drug they are. Thus the name amphetamine sulphate is the group name for the drug whose full chemical name is alpha-methylphenethyl-amine. The trade name tells you where the drug comes from, i.e. who its manufacturer is. The trade name Benzedrine refers to the particular brand of amphetamine sulphate manufactured by Smith, Kline and French Ltd. (a drug-manufacturing firm).

Drinamyl looks like many other small round pills. They are known today as 'blues'. The other drug of this group which has become widely misused is *Durophet*, made by Riker Laboratories. This drug comes in several capsule forms. The 12.5 milligram capsule is coloured black and white and has become known as 'black and white'. The 20 milligram capsule is all black, and this is the famous 'black bomber'. There are other varieties coloured differently.

'Pep pills' in general are often referred to as 'sweets' 'jelly-beans' and the person who takes them as a 'pill-head'.

Methylamphetamine (Methedrine) is a very powerful stimulant. It was synthesised in 1919 in Japan and has been used in Britain since 1940 in hospitals, in spinal anaesthesia and for raising the blood pressure after severe operations. When abused, it leads to serious paranoid psychoses. Unlike other amphetamines, it is normally injected. (See Note 1, page 40.)

Being under the influence of pills is described as being 'blocked', and the effect can be serious. They do not produce what we have termed physical dependence, but they can lead to hallucinations and severe mental changes. The user will find that, in order to maintain the effect of the pill, he needs to increase the dose. Sometimes the effect of large quantities of amphetamines is clinically indistinguishable from the mental illness known as *schizophrenia*. In small quantities, amphetamines lessen fatigue and increase wakefulness, suppress hunger, raise the blood pressure, increase talkativeness, but also lead to palpitations, instability, and headache.

Pep pills circulate widely in most towns. Their prices vary according to the type. The traffic is fed from three main sources: (1) over-prescription by doctors, and forged prescriptions; (2) thefts from manufacturers' warehouses and chemists' shops; (3) illicit manufacture and imports from overseas. Today the massive over-prescribing by some doctors has been very much reduced, and in some areas, such as Ipswich, there has been a voluntary ban on prescribing. There are probably fewer pills of this type around now on the teenage illicit market than was the case in the mid-1960s, but it is still fairly easy to obtain them in many towns. In 1965 3.8 million prescriptions for amphetamines alone were issued on the National Health Service, and this figure probably covered some 100,000,000 tablets. Again, one pharmacist, on the basis of his own survey, estimated that between May 1966 and the end of that year, at least 80 pharmacies were broken into, and amphetamine drugs were the main drugs stolen. Miss Alice Bacon (a Minister at the Home Office) said in January 1967 that, in July 1966, 250,000 tablets had been stolen from a warehouse. In December 1966, 117 people were charged with possessing 73,620 tablets and capsules, and of these, six people held between them 62,214 tablets, and 55 people each had 20 tablets or fewer.

Sedatives, Hypnotics and Tranquillizers

The Brain Committee in 1961 accepted the following definition of the drugs of this type:

'A *sedative* is a drug which depresses the central nervous system especially at higher levels so as to allay nervousness, anxiety, fear and excitement, but not normally to the extent of inducing sleep. A *hypnotic* is a drug used to induce sleep which does so by depression of the central nervous system more profoundly than a sedative but with a restricted duration of effect. A *tranquillizer* is a drug which promotes a sense of calmness or well-being without that degree of depression on the central nervous system commonly associated with the sedatives or hypnotics .

The barbiturates are hypnotics which depress the central nervous system: there are other non-barbiturate hypnotics whose effects are less severe, though abuse of them can be dangerous. The use of these substances has recently increased.

In 1970 no less than 16.2 million National Health prescriptions were issued for barbiturate drugs, and they constitute a serious problem. In 1934, a Home Office expert described barbiturates as holding 'the foremost place amongst the drugs of addiction'. The number of prescriptions has been increasing over the years. In 1934 they formed just over 1 per cent of total prescriptions, but by 1947 they had risen to 4.6 per cent. What has caused alarm, too, is the increase in deaths from barbiturates. In 1965 there were 1,490 suicides and 525 accidental deaths from barbiturates. Since 1965 the number of suicides and accidental deaths from these drugs has doubled. The most popular of the barbiturate drugs prescribed is phenobarbitone, followed by Amytal, Soneryl, Nembutal and Seconal.

Cannabis

Cannabis sativa is the name of the hemp plant. 'Marijuana' is a popular name given to the drug derived from the top of the plant, 'hashish' to the pure resin. The effects of hashish (also known as Indian hemp or 'weed') are more potent than those of marijuana (also known as 'pot', 'weed', 'tea', 'charge', 'grass', etc.) because the resin contains more of the active chemical principles. Both are smoked in 'joints' or 'reefers', and to be in possession of either is a criminal offence. Under the new Misuse of Drugs Act it is an offence for an occupier of premises to allow production, supply or smoking of cannabis. 'Permitting' means allowing any person to smoke cannabis at any time, whereas the old Act merely referred to permitting premises to be used 'for the purpose' of smoking cannabis.

Cannabis has been used in various countries from ancient times. Herodotus, one of the greatest historians of ancient Greece (484–424 B.C.) mentions the use of hashish by the Scythians, though it was used for cleansing purposes, and not for pleasure. It is sanctioned by the Hindu and Islamic religions which forbid alcohol, and its use is widespread throughout India, Pakistan, North Africa, and parts of Latin America. It gives the user a feeling of well-being, contentment, relaxation, and pleasant drowsiness. He may appear intoxicated, and laugh and giggle excessively, and there may be hallucinations. But there are also adverse effects: extreme nervousness, anxiety and hysteria, and in some cases, psychotic illness. Being under the influence of cannabis is called being 'stoned'.

The effects of Cannabis

It should be noted that hashish, while it produces the same kind of effects, is stronger and longer lasting than marijuana. There is disagreement about the effects of the drug, and there are two over-simplified attitudes.

First there are those who say that cannabis is addictive and dangerous, who connect cannabis with violent crime, insanity, promiscuity and even the overthrow of the western world. Such wild claims are made more frequently in the United States, but one often encounters them in Britain in conversation.

Secondly there are those who argue that cannabis is less harmful than alcohol and less habit-forming than tobacco. Among these, some would encourage the use of cannabis as an aid to relaxation, reducing nervous tension and inhibitions. Others would simply claim that it is a pleasure-giving drug which has few seriously adverse effects.

Both these attitudes contain elements of truth, but they overstate the case and oversimplify the problem. It is important to try and look at the effects of cannabis as honestly, freely and calmly as we can.

First, let us clear away some of the myths about cannabis,

relying on the views and experience of experts, not on the often ignorant opinions expressed in the press. Cannabis is not an addictive drug. Two American psychiatrists, S. Allentuck and K. M. Bowman who, in 1942, studied the effects of cannabis, stressed that 'the psychic habituation to marijuana is not as strong as tobacco or alcohol'. A World Health Organization study in 1964 reached the conclusion that there was no *physical dependence* on the drug. A WHO expert, Dr. Joel Fort of the University of California has said 'No physical dependency occurs, although with chronic excessive use psychic dependency and toxic effects can occur. With ordinary doses there is no scientific evidence of harmfulness to the individual or to society'. Nor does it of itself increase sex drive, as is often claimed; what it does is to release inhibitions, as alcohol does, and it often reduces sex drive. It does not of itself lead to crime. In the USA the leading authority, Dr. Donald Louria, says that 'there is no evidence that the use of marijuana results in criminal activity'.

In Britain, Dr. P. A. L. Chapple has said that 'psychiatrists have been unable to show an association between cannabis and major crime'. Nor does smoking cannabis automatically lead the user to more dangerous drugs. This is often claimed, and it is so important that we shall discuss it more fully later. We should note, however, that our knowledge of the psychological and physiological effects of the drug is very incomplete. We should not pretend to know more than we do. But, so far as our present knowledge goes, it is true to say that cannabis is not addictive, and does not lead automatically, either to crime or to more dangerous drugs.

On the other hand, it is believed by many experts that there is such a thing as 'dependence' upon cannabis. The widespread view that there is no danger in the use of cannabis is certainly false. As we said above, it can lead to severe anxiety and to the serious mental condition known as *psychosis*. It can also lead the user to be dependent on the drug. This is not real *addiction*, in which there is *biological* dependence and effects on the body, but it is more a habit formed by experience of pleasant sensations. Thus, the leading British authority, Dr. Max Glatt, points out: 'In this country we have had a number of cases of people becoming psychologically dependent on it'. (*The Guardian*, 9 February 1967.)

In 1969 the Government Advisory Committee on Drug Dependence produced its report *Cannabis*. This has become known as the Wootton Report, and it confirms most of the facts stated here. (See Note 2, page 40.) Since then, there has been a steady flow of research material on cannabis, particularly from the United States. While many of the old myths have been demolished, there is still a good deal of concern about the effect of the drug on the maturing process in adolescence, on driving and, in the case of heavy use, on mental function.

'Escalation'

It is often said, however, that the chief danger in the use of cannabis does not lie in the drug itself, but in the fact that it leads the user to more dangerous drugs, such as heroin. This has become known as the 'escalation' thesis. The user, it is claimed, moves on from the 'soft' to the 'hard' drug. Is there any truth in this view?

First, it is a fact that almost all heroin addicts *have* at some time used cannabis.

Why do they go on to heroin? Some addicts say that cannabis could not maintain its effect, so they went on to something better. But on the whole, it is the very disturbed who turn to heroin, and they would probably have turned to heroin even if cannabis had not existed. Studies in prison have shown that heroin addicts tend to have a history of emotional disturbance prior to their addiction, whereas cannabis offenders are on the whole of 'normal' personality.

It is sometimes argued that because cannabis is illegal, those who wish to use it must go to criminals, and that through such contacts they may meet the pushers of heroin. But in fact, the sources of supply are not on the whole the same. If the cannabis user 'escalates', it is more likely to be to LSD rather than heroin. In fact, most cannabis users do not go on to other drugs.

For, secondly, it is clear that the escalation thesis falls down on examination. If cannabis did lead its users on to heroin, by now we would have hundreds of thousands of heroin addicts in the country. In fact, heroin has probably declined while cannabis use has been increasing. The truth is that cannabis is part of the background out of which the drug addict emerges, but there is no more reason to say that it leads to heroin than to say that, because most methylated spirit addicts have started on beer, beer leads to meths. This is plainly absurd.

Cannabis needs to be examined and assessed in relation to the known facts, not on the basis of false claims and fears. Further research may well reveal that there are dangers of which we are at present unaware. But it is important not to be carried away by hysteria and not to distort the situation.

LSD

Lysergic Acid Diethylamide is an hallucinatory drug. It brings about changes in the biochemistry of the brain, and can lead to serious mental upheavals. LSD has become known as a 'psychedelic' or mind-expanding drug, and its devotees see it as a blessing, a drug which can enrich our lives and bring new spiritual experiences. The leading exponent of this view is Dr. Timothy Leary, a former professor at Harvard Medical School, in the United States of America, Leary at one time claimed some 50,000 disciples in the USA, and his 'League of Spiritual Discovery' stresses the religious value of LSD. In Britain, Aldous Huxley's praise of Mescalin in his *The Doors of Perception* came near to Leary's psychedelic cult. In the early 1950s some British psychiatrists claimed that LSD had great value in therapy, particularly in helping patients to recover long-forgotten memories of early childhood. One of these doctors, Dr. A. M. Spencer, claimed, 'The doctor uses this to free the patient from those fears and disturbed relationships of early childhood which have crippled him emotionally and resulted in his neurotic illness'. The doctor can then effect a cure.

Since the early days of Leary's claims, the spiritual value of LSD has been questioned by some leading authorities on mysticism, especially by the Indian mystic Meher Baba. 'The search for truth through drugs', he says, 'must end in disillusionment'. On LSD he comments, 'although LSD is not a physically addicting drug, one can become attached to the *experiences* arising from its use, and one gets tempted to use it in increased doses, again and again, in the hope of deeper and deeper experiences. But this can only lead to madness'.

However, leaving aside the therapeutic and clinical values of the drug, there is no doubt that its irresponsible use, and the spread of an illicit market in Britain as well as in the USA has very grave dangers. William Burroughs, author of *The Naked Lunch* and *Junkie*, has written about LSD and drugs of the psychedelic group, 'I consider these drugs more dangerous than useful . . . Under no circumstances would I use any of these drugs at the present time, or advise anyone else to do so'. An American psychologist, Dr. Allan Cohen, says that the psychedelic subculture 'contains the seeds of its own destruction'. The chemical approach to the expansion of consciousness, he claims, is artificial; if the user does not later turn to more positive avenues, his capacity for productive existence is reduced.

LSD taken without medical supervision can be disastrous. It may induce extraordinary mental aberrations, and psychotic delusions which may last for days, or may lead either to chronic psychosis, temporary or permanent damage to the central nervous system, or death. Even very small amounts are dangerous, since a fraction of an ounce can provide 10,000 doses. It is colourless, odourless, and tasteless, easy to manufacture and even easier to conceal. The danger of its use in chemical warfare is obvious and terrifying

In August 1966, the UN Commission on Narcotic Drugs recommended immediate action by governments to control the production, distribution and use of LSD, and similar drugs. In September, the Committee on the Safety of Drugs (the Dunlop Committee) in Britain asked the main suppliers of the drug, Brocades, a Czechoslovakian firm, to sell only to approved psychiatrists, though this restriction was slightly eased later. (Earlier, in April, the American firm, Sandoz, with headquarters in Switzerland, had announced their decision to cease manufacturing the drug.) The drug was added to the list of controlled drugs but it has continued to be illicitly manufactured and has spread throughout the country.

Since 1967 the word 'psychedelic' has spread rapidly from the rather restricted circle of LSD users, and has become an 'in-word' used loosely about clothes, art, music, and so on – rather in the sense that the words 'kinky' and 'groovy' are used. This is a good example of how the popularising of a word loses some of the key points of its original meaning. Psychedelic has now been taken over by commercial interests, and shops advertise their 'psychedelic gear'. In his book *The Psychedelic Experience*, Timothy Leary tried to define the word in this way:

A psychedelic experience is a journey to new realms of consciousness. The scope and content of the experience is limitless, but its characteristic features are the transcendence of verbal concepts or space-time dimensions, and of the ego or identity. Such experience of enlarged identity can occur in a variety of ways: sensory deprivation, yoga exercises, disciplined meditation, religious or aesthetic ecstasies, or spontaneously. Most recently they have become available to anyone through the ingestion of psychedelic drugs.

Here psychedelic refers to something which enlarges our experience of reality. But the experience is often described as bringing light and brilliance, and so in popular jargon 'psychedelic' has come to be associated with vivid startling colours, and fascinating musical sounds. Leary, for example, has said:

But when your nervous system is turned on with LSD and all the wires are flashing, the senses begin to overlap and merge. You not only hear but *see* the music emerging from the speaker system – like dancing particles, like squirming curls of toothpaste. You actually *see* the sound, in multi-coloured patterns, while you're hearing it. At the same time, you *are* the sound, you are the note, you are the string of the violin or piano.

Two other drugs, similar to LSD are also used in order to bring about the psychedelic experience. They are called DMT (Dimethyltriptamine) and STP (methyldimethoxy-alpha-methylphenylethylamine). The effect of STP is similar to that of some nerve gases used in chemical warfare. It can lead to a psychotic state more dangerous and more lasting than that produced by LSD, and if a patient, after using STP, is treated in hospital with the drug Largactil to quieten him, he may die. The psychedelic experience often leads not to heavenly bliss, as expected by the user, but to pure hell and to insanity or death.

Drug Traffic

The traffic in drugs differs in its nature according to the type of drug involved. We shall see in later pages that the traffic in heroin has been largely fed by 'over-prescription'; the amphetamine pusher relies on large-scale thefts, while the marijuana and hashish traffic is international. A UN report in 1965 said that it 'continues to be, in quantitative terms, the biggest narcotic substance in illicit traffic'.

There have been many cases of large quantities of cannabis smuggled into Britain. One of the biggest was 119 lb (valued at a black market price of £42,000) brought into Dover in 1966. But most of the marijuana comes from small, unorganized contacts. Students returning from holidays in North Africa have played an important part in the passing of the drug in recent years.

The traffickers in amphetamines often operate small, well-organized cliques of pushers. They are unscrupulous and often dangerous men, concerned for their own profits, and unconcerned at the misery they create. Their victims are the youngsters who are often referred to as the 'unattached'. These include a 'hard core' of rootless and homeless kids who are in the cafes and clubs of London and other cities on most nights, and also the vast majority of 'weekenders'. Most of these are basically stable, and their involvement in drugs is one part of their adolescent experimentation. They grow out of it and leave it behind them. But some are less fortunate; they become 'hooked' or dependent on pills – they become 'pill-heads'.

In many cases, it is coffee bars and coffee clubs which are the scenes of the pill traffic. It is easy to become unbalanced about this and exaggerate its seriousness. Of course, many coffee clubs are dangerous and unhealthy, but many others are cheerful, healthy, and perform a very valuable function in the social life of teenagers.

Some Myths about Drugs and Drug Traffic

It is often said that coloured immigrants have been responsible for the increase in drug addiction in Britain.

This is quite untrue. It is certainly a fact that until recently most of the convictions for possession of marijuana were of persons of West Indian and West African origin, that is, persons from countries where the drug was commonly grown and used; but in the last few years there have been more and more English people convicted. There is no evidence that coloured immigrants have contributed in any other way to the drug problem in Britain. Almost all the traffic in amphetamines is carried on by English people. And there are hardly any coloured addicts on hard drugs. (If any immigrant group stands out significantly in the heroin field, it is the Canadian.)

Again, many people believe that it is only (or mainly) art students, poets, 'beatniks', 'weirdies' and 'hippies' who take drugs. This is not true. Drug takers are drawn from every group and class. There have been more middle-class than working-class addicts to heroin in the past, but this is changing. Again, the smoking of marijuana was once confined to certain groups, but this is no longer the case. Drug misuse is spread through all sections of British society.

Nor is it true that all or most drug takers are 'juvenile delinquents' or criminals. Many are delinquent, many are on the criminal fringe. But there are many more who are not.

In short, many of the generalizations and myths about drug taking are based on a failure to take all the facts into account. The subject lends itself to hysteria, panic and irresponsibility. As students of the subject, it is our duty not to be led astray by these false attitudes, but to examine the facts.

QUESTIONS FOR DISCUSSION

1. What do we mean by 'the drug problem', and how do you think it should be tackled?
   (a) by the Press;

    (b) by schools, churches and youth clubs;
    (c) by individuals?

2. Explain the differences between the types of drugs which are misused in Britain today.
3. What are 'pep pills' and what are their effects?
4. Do you think cannabis smoking is beneficial or harmful, and why?
   Is there a case for legalizing cannabis?
5. Why do some young people progress from pills and cannabis to heroin?
6. Do you think that LSD has a place in the life of the future generation?
7. How can we best combat the drug traffic?
8. Are coloured people to blame for drug traffic in Britain?

Note 1. Intravenous Use of Amphetamines

Between 1966 and 1968 there was an epidemic, particularly in London, of intravenous use of methylamphetamine (Methedrine). When this drug was restricted by an agreement between the Ministry of Health and the manufacturers (October 1968), there was an increase in the use of other amphetamines, as well as sedatives and hypnotic drugs, by injection.

Note 2. The Wootton Report 1969

The Report of the Standing Advisory Committee on Drug Dependence entitled *Cannabis* (popularly known as the Wootton Report) was published in 1969. It is a balanced and informative study of the evidence about the use of cannabis, and contains important recommendations about penalties and legislation. Because the Report has been misrepresented in the press, it is most important that it should be studied in full. It can be obtained from Her Majesty's Stationery Office.

4

HEROIN ADDICTION

Heroin

HEROIN is derived from opium and is known as an *opiate*. Opium itself comes from a plant of the poppy family and has been used in medicine for hundreds of years. It was in 1830 that a German pharmacist separated a main ingredient of opium, morphine, and a few years later another natural opium alkaloid, codeine, was identified. Both these drugs can lead to addiction, but codeine is less potent than morphine.

The full name of heroin is *diacetylmorphine* or diamorphine, and it is a synthetic alkaloid produced by heating morphine and acetic acid. It is more potent and more quickly addictive than morphine. Heroin was introduced in 1898 and has been used for the relief of pain. Since then, pharmacists have been trying to find an equally effective pain-killer which is also non-addictive.

The effect of heroin is mainly *depressant*: that is, it lowers the level of nervous and other bodily activity. Immediately after an injection or 'fix', the user gets 'high' and feels a sense of relaxation and freedom from this world and its problems. His appetite will be reduced, and so will his sex drive, and for a long period he will nod and doze and appear to be aimless, drowsy, but peaceful. But for those heavily addicted, there is no such 'high': the heroin for them simply helps them to escape the terror of physical illness, which would result if they did not have their 'fix'.

Two main physical dangers of using heroin are *overdose* and *infection*. An overdose occurs when the amount of heroin injected into the vein exceeds the physical tolerance of the body, and such an overdose can be fatal. Infection results from unsterile needles which may be shared among several addicts. In fact, mortality among heroin addicts in Britain is around 22 deaths per thousand per year, a higher ratio than in the United States. About a third of all heroin addicts admitted to hospital are known to have shared syringes with other addicts, and there has been an increase in the numbers of addicts suffering from a liver disease called 'infectious hepatitis'. Even the use of an unsterile needle on one occasion can lead to permanent liver damage.

Heroin is used in four ways: orally, sniffing, by injection into the skin ('skin-popping'), and by injection into the bloodstream ('main-lining'). In order to get a greater kick, it is combined with *cocaine*, a stimulant derived from coca leaves, and the combination is known as 'H and C' or 'speedball'. Very few people in Britain use cocaine alone, and the use of cocaine by addicts has sharply declined.

A young addict may begin by 'skin-popping' and soon progress to 'main-lining'. Main-lining is less expensive since it requires a smaller amount of heroin than skin-popping. The addict will use a specified amount of heroin and cocaine. Heroin, in Britain, is manufactured in small white tablets, each one being one-sixth of a grain. Sterile water can be bought in ampoules, but most addicts use ordinary water from taps or lavatories (and not, therefore, germ free). The heroin is dissolved in water and injected by a hypodermic syringe into the bloodstream. In order to inject, a 'tourniquet' is used. This may be a scarf, belt, handkerchief or tie and is wrapped round the arm tightly until a vein is found. Some addicts find a vein at once without difficulty; others sweat and scream and endure great suffering of mind and body.

As the veins are used over and over again for injection, they become scarred and unusable. As the larger veins collapse, the addict will turn to smaller veins in arms or hands, and then may go on to use leg veins. If a long-standing main-liner runs out of usable veins, he may return to skin-popping, and this can lead to multiple sores under the skin and perhaps to tetanus.

The use of heroin causes a constriction of the pupils of the eyes – that is, the pupils become smaller. The addict will also appear to be frequently drowsy and may nod off to sleep in the middle of conversation. These factors, plus the presence of needle marks and scars and perhaps boils and abscesses, make recognition of a heroin addict fairly easy. But the most terrible visible sign of an addict is the 'withdrawal symptoms' which occur when, for some reason, his supply of drugs ceases. 'Withdrawal symptoms' can be very violent and painful, and include running nose, cramp, sexual orgasm, vomiting, yawning, and sometimes epilepsy.

What exactly does heroin do to the human body? After an injection a good deal of the morphine content becomes concentrated in the liver and kidneys. The effect of the drug on nervous activity is usually described as depressant (as we said above) but it can excite and stimulate as well. However, it has been argued that most of the physical and mental harm attributed to heroin is, in fact, due not to the drug itself but to the indirect results of its use – loss of appetite, lack of cleanliness, and so on. Others have claimed that more harm to the body has been the result of cocaine which injured the central nervous system and made the body more open to injury (as do the amphetamines). Today few 'needle addicts' use cocaine, but many use crushed barbiturates, and these, more than heroin, can cause very severe physical damage. In fact it is the whole way of life of the addict, his personality problems, his relation to and rejection by society, rather than the heroin itself, which brings about the most terrible tragedies. One British psychiatrist, Dr. J. H. Willis, for instance, has stressed that 'there is surprisingly little evidence that narcotic addiction is intrinsically destructive, either physically or psychologically'. What is destructive is the vicious circle produced by the combined effects of drug, personality, and society. It is the combination of these factors, rather than the drugs alone, which makes addiction so serious a problem and so often, apparently, an insoluble one.

The numbers of addicts in Britain

It is believed by many people that there have been 'registered drug addicts' for many years. This, in fact, was not the case until 1967, when the Dangerous Drugs Bill introduced a system of compulsory notification. What happened previously was that addicts of restricted dangerous drugs became known to the Drugs Branch of the Home Office. First, if they received heroin and cocaine on prescription, their names were noted during regular inspections of pharmacists' registers. Secondly, if they were receiving supplies illicitly from a 'pusher', they became known through police action. The Home Office figures were often criticised as being under-estimates. In fact, they were not estimates at all, but accurate records of *known addicts*.* Even today there are many who are unknown; these include those who receive supplies from the surplus of other addicts and have escaped the notice of the police. You can see youngsters in the West End of London and elsewhere trying to buy heroin from addicts. Most young addicts have, in fact, started in this way: they buy small amounts from an addict's surplus. They subsequently find that they need more of the drug, and they register with a clinic. But many addicts prefer to buy heroin on the illicit market rather

* These records include only those persons who have received drugs in any given year, in contrast to the USA, where the Federal Bureau of Narcotics keep the names of known addicts for five years.

than 'register', believing that once they have registered, they are really 'hooked' and known to the authorities.

The table below shows the increase in the numbers of addicts known to the Home Office in recent years and the ages of these addicts:

DRUG ADDICTS KNOWN TO THE HOME OFFICE 1962–1968

	1962	1963	1964	1965	1966	1967	1968	1969	1970	1971
Totals addicts	532	635	753	927	1349	1729	2782	2881	2661	2769
Total using heroin	175	237	342	521	899	1299	2240	1417	914	959
Age Structure										
Under 20	3	17	40	145	329	395	764	637	405	338
20-34	132	184	257	347	558	906	1530	1789	1813	2010
35-49	107	128	138	134	162	142	146	174	158	156
50 and over	274	298	311	291	286	279	260	241	253	226
Unknown	16	8	7	10	14	7	82	40	32	39
Total	532	635	753	927	1349	1729	2782	2881	2661	2769

NOTE
1. The figures represent the total number of all addicts who have come to notice during each year. Since 1969 the Home Office have also kept records of those still addicted on the last day of each year, and these figures are much smaller.
2. The 1969-71 totals for heroin do not include those using heroin and methadone.

The heroin epidemic reached its peak in 1968. In that year, out of 2782 known addicts, 2240 were on heroin, and 764 were under 20, including ten aged 15 and forty aged 16, all but three on heroin. Three characteristics of the increase are very important. First, its speed. When the Brain Committee produced its First Report in 1961 it claimed that 'on the evidence before us the incidence of addiction to dangerous drugs was very small', and that 'there seemed no reason to think that any increase was occurring'. By the time the Committee was reconvened in 1964 the position had changed drastically. Secondly, the fact that the greatest increase was in heroin, associated at different periods with the intravenous use of cocaine and Methedrine. The number of new heroin addicts from 1955 to 1964 followed a smoothly increasing curve, doubling approximately every nineteen months. After 1969, however, the heroin figures started to drop. Thirdly, the fact that the new addicts were all in the young age group. There were no known teenage addicts at all before 1960. By 1965 there were 145 of whom 134 were on heroin, and the total figure had risen to 329 in 1966. The 20–34 age group, too, showed increases from 50 in 1959 to 347 in 1965, 319 of these being on heroin. The average age of heroin addicts fell between 1960 and 1964 from 28.7 to 23.5 years. There is some evidence now that heroin addiction may be declining, although it is too early to be certain.

It is sometimes claimed that a large percentage of British addicts are, themselves, doctors and nurses. This is not really accurate. It is true that there has been for some years a fairly stable group of 'medical addicts' but the evidence suggests that the number of these is decreasing. Nor is it entirely true to say that British addicts come from the upper and middle classes. A study of addicts treated at St. Bernard's Hospital, Southall, between 1959 and 1965 showed that the majority did *not* come from these classes. Recently, in fact, there has been a marked increase in the numbers of working-class addicts of heroin. The majority, too, are what are called *non-therapeutic* addicts as opposed to therapeutic addicts (i.e. those who become addicted to a drug after having been prescribed it in the course of treatment for illness). Another feature of the recent growth is the predominance of male addicts. The new cases of heroin addiction recorded from 1960 to 1964 for British subjects included 200 males (70 per cent) and only 81 females. In 1965, out of the total of 927 addicts known to the Home Office, 558 (60 per cent) were male. Most of them are probably not married, since addiction makes a normal sex life impossible for most people.

It is difficult to prophesy what may happen in the future. On the one hand, there seems no basis for the view that drug addiction will totally disappear. On the other hand, there is no doubt that intravenous use of heroin, methadone and barbiturates has only affected a small percentage of the total drug-using population. The use of drugs by injection is not, mercifully, attractive to most young people.

How Britain differs from the United States

In Britain an addict is recognised by the law and by the medical profession as a sick person. He is not a criminal unless he breaks the law in order to get his supplies. In 1926 a committee of medical men, called the Rolleston Committee, laid down certain principles, which have become known as the 'Rolleston principles'. They interpreted our Dangerous Drugs Law to mean that an addict was a sick person and should be allowed the dosage of drug necessary for normal functioning.

In the United States, before the Harrison Act of 1914, anyone could buy drugs from his local 'drug store'. After the Act, the police began to suppress the use of narcotics, and by the 1920s there had grown up a flourishing drug underworld. By the early 1950s, when there seemed to be only a very slight heroin problem in this country, a special narcotics court in Chicago dealt with over 6,000 cases in five months. The American market is fed by international criminal syndicates. France has become an important middle point in the organization of traffic between the Middle East and America. While there are relatively few drug addicts in France, it is in a good position for the flow of opium derivatives from Afghanistan, Iran, Turkey and elsewhere, to the United States. Opium will arrive in France, either in its crude state or already transformed into morphine. The process of manufacturing heroin goes on in several clandestine factories, the exact location of which move about as police activity intensifies. Observers say that the specialists tend to be Southern French, and often Corsican.

The heroin which is used in the criminal industry is in *powder* form, and it is because of this that traffic in heroin is so profitable, since it is diluted and mixed with other substances. (Until recently there was no evidence that powder heroin had been circulating in Britain, but it made its appearance in 1967.) The heroin used in the American black market trade is therefore considerably weaker than that used in Britain. It is mixed with milk, sugar or quinine, and by the time it reaches the addict it has been estimated that the five dollar street packet contains five grains of five per cent heroin. The profits from the smuggling, diluting and selling of heroin in the United States have been said to be between 350,000,000 and 700,000,000 dollars per year. Large scale syndicates are involved.

We see already that there are two important differences between the United States and Britain. First, the heroin itself differs in its form and strength. Secondly, the heroin traffic in the United States is an organized criminal industry. In Britain, on the other hand, successive reports from the Home Office to the United Nations have stressed that there has been very little organized illicit traffic, and that all the heroin circulating on the 'black market' has come on prescription.

A third difference is the fact that in the United States, heroin addiction is closely tied up with delinquent activity and is concentrated in certain districts, areas of decayed slums and poverty. There are districts which are recognizable as 'addict quarters'. Most American addicts come from the economically deprived groups and live in zones of bad housing and social distress. If you read the small study by Jeremy Larner and Ralph Tefferteller, *The Addict in the Street* (Penguin, 1966) you will see how close is the link between heroin addiction and run-down slum districts. One of the addicts interviewed in the book explained, 'Harlem is the center-point for narcotics in the New York area. From 100th Street to 140th Street is narcotics row'. Another one claimed 'there are probably fifty thousand addicts in colored Harlem alone'.

A group called Harlem Youth Opportunities Unlimited (HARYOU) made a study of this district in 1964. Twenty per cent of the housing units are overcrowded and there is a great lack of community services. The juvenile delinquency rate is more than twice as high as that for New York City as a whole. The HARYOU report claimed that 'it is the consensus of opinion . . . that between 40 and 60 per cent of the 60,000 addicts in the United States live in New York City' and that the rate of narcotics users reported in Central Harlem between 1955 and 1961 'is consistently about ten times as high as the rate for the city as a whole'. A more detailed study by a group of sociologists under Isidor Chein in 1963 had shown that Harlem had the highest rate of juvenile drug misuse and that 'the areas of highest drug use include some of the city's worst slums'.

Official figures from the Federal Bureau of Narcotics in the United States show that in December 1964 there were 55,899 known drug addicts in the country, compared with 48,535 in 1963. 10,012 of these were new cases. 78.5 per cent of all addicts were concentrated in ten cities, of which New York had the most (28,098). 5.2 of the addicts in New York were under 21, compared with 3.6 for the USA as a whole, and 50.6 per cent aged between 21 and 30, compared with 46.7 per cent for the USA as a whole. Of the total of 55,899 addicts, 51,634 were heroin addicts. Today there are probably about 350,000 heroin addicts in the United States.

A fourth difference, allied to the third, is the fact that in the United States a large proportion of addicts are non-white. In 1964 the Federal Bureau of Narcotics reported that over half of known addicts under 30 years of age were Negro, while 18 per cent were Puerto Rican or Mexican, and only 28 per cent were white. There are two state hospitals which treat voluntary and convict addicts: Lexington, Kentucky, and Fort Worth, Texas. Addicts from Alabama, Georgia and Kentucky, the hospitals report, are 90 per cent white, but these tend to be old-style morphine addicts. The newer addicts are much younger and most of them are Puerto Rican.

The contrast with Britain is clear. The British addicts do not come in general from run-down slum districts, although there are signs that some slum districts are developing a heroin problem; nor do they come from a minority ethnic group. There are very few coloured addicts in Britain. Of the 709 heroin addicts in the United Kingdom who were first known to be addicted between 1955 and 1965, 587 were British born, and 72 were Canadian, nineteen were American, ten Jamaican, seven Australian, and other nationalities, nine in all, totalled 14. Again, it is true to say that in Britain heroin has not so far become tied up with the growth of criminal areas or 'ghettoes' of inequality and decay. This is not to say that such areas will not arise in Britain, and there are clearly real dangers in some of our 'twilight zones', the slum districts of big cities.

Two further comments on the American scene are important. First, it seems that the length of addiction in the United States is not very great. The Federal Bureau of Narcotics has, since 1953, kept the names of known addicts in an 'active' list for five years after they are reported. It has been found that, while addicts come in yearly, the *total* number did not increase during the 1950s. Two-thirds of the addicts seem to have become inactive in their mid-thirties, and the average length of addiction was 8.6 years. It has been said, therefore, that many addicts 'mature out' of addiction. Secondly, experience of American legislation has led many to favour a more *permissive* attitude to addiction, while in Britain the present trend seems to be towards a more restrictive policy. It is precisely now that the Americans are beginning to question the value of their 'system' that Britain seems to be showing some signs of moving in an American direction.

The Sources for Heroin

We have said that heroin addicts in Britain can obtain supplies from doctors at clinics. In theory, until the coming into effect of the Dangerous Drugs Act 1967, any doctor was free to prescribe heroin, but in practice very few were willing to do so. There were three main reasons for this. First, many doctors had serious conscientious scruples about prescribing a drug which they knew was slowly killing their patient; they believed that by doing so they were co-operating in an act of suicide. Secondly, doctors realized that one heroin addict might take up as much time and energy as the rest of their patients put together. Not only this, but he would come late for appointments, or come in the middle of the night – and he would bring other addicts with him. Thirdly, after 1965, many doctors were under the impression that the Ministry of Health, which had promised to open special 'treatment centres', was discouraging doctors from prescribing these drugs. (More will be said later about this aspect.)

For these reasons, the number of doctors who prescribed for and helped heroin addicts became very small. One of them, writing in February, 1966, said: 'It is exceedingly difficult for an addict to obtain acceptance on a doctor's National Health Service list. At present, in consequence, addicts living all over London can only find a very few doctors to take them on, often much farther away than the area usually covered by a general practice'. He went on to point out that this situation added to the difficulties of the few doctors who did treat addicts. A report published in August 1964 on experience of treating 100 addicts showed that 35 addicts in a total National Health Service list of 3,500 required during a busy month (January, 1964) a quarter of all items of service in surgery time. Thus one per cent of the patients in this surgery produced twenty per cent of the doctor's work. This estimate, the doctor explained, left out telephone calls from addicts at inconvenient times (such as the middle of the night), calls from chemists and police, reports to courts, dealing with the Home Office, and so on. Addicts take time, energy, and patience, and it is not surprising that very few doctors are willing to cope with them.

Dr. E. M. Schur, an American sociologist who studied addiction in Britain, found that in 1959 13 doctors in the London area were the main source of heroin for addicts. Of the doctors who prescribed heroin, there were, perhaps, three categories. First, those who worked closely with hospital units and who, accepting the fact that they themselves could not cure addiction, would prescribe only on the understanding that the patient was prepared for hospital treatment. Secondly, those who tried not only to prescribe but to treat and help the addict to 'come off' and who therefore saw their role as therapeutic, that is, concerned with healing. (This would also at some stage include getting the patient into hospital.) Thirdly, those who were concerned simply to make money out of prescribing heroin privately (i.e. outside the National Health Service) and who did not help the addict at all.

In 1968, general practitioners were forbidden to prescribe heroin and/or cocaine for addicts, and out-patient treatment was restricted to new 'treatment centres'. This action was the result of factors which will now be described.

The Brain Report

When the Brain Committee reported for the second time in 1965 they claimed that 'there is at present no evidence of any significant traffic, organized or otherwise, in dangerous drugs that have been stolen or smuggled into this country' (paragraph 9). They added that forgery and deception had not added very much to the amount of available drugs. They then went on to say:

> From the evidence before us we have been led to the conclusion that the major source of supply has been the activity of a very few doctors who have prescribed excessively for addicts (paragraph 11).
> The evidence further shows that not more than six doctors have prescribed these very large amounts of dangerous drugs for individual patients . . . (paragraph 12).

As a result the Brain Committee went on to recommend (paragraph 16) that special restrictions should be applied to heroin and cocaine. They recommended that all addicts be notified to a central authority (paragraph 18) and that specialized treatment centres should be set up as soon as possible (paragraph 22) especially in London. Only doctors on the staff of such centres should, in future, be allowed to prescribe heroin and cocaine, and offending doctors should be dealt with by the Disciplinary Committee of the General Medical Council (paragraphs 26–36).

The Brain Report, unfortunately, had a number of serious and bad effects. First, the number of doctors willing to prescribe heroin for addicts dwindled after the publication of the Report. Some of the old doctors were angry and strongly resented the apparent condemnation of their work. Secondly, new doctors were reluctant to enter a field which they realized they would soon be compelled to leave. Thirdly, a few unscrupulous doctors 'cashed in' on this very difficult and dangerous situation, and began to prescribe heroin and cocaine to very large numbers of addicts, and to charge them for each prescription.

The fact that the treatment centres had still not appeared eighteen months after the Report had been published meant that the position had become progressively worse instead of better. It was not until near the end of 1966 that an Advisory Committee on Drug Dependence was set up. In 1967 the Dangerous Drugs Bill was introduced into and passed through Parliament: this made it an offence for a general practitioner to prescribe heroin and cocaine for addicts except in emergencies unless he had a licence to do so, and so put into effect one of the principles of the Brain Report.

The dangers for the future

The main danger for the future is that, as heroin becomes harder to obtain from medical sources, so the black market will develop. We need to be very careful about the use of the term 'black market'. In one sense it is true to say that there has been no real black market in Britain until very recently. What was happening was that addicts were getting more heroin from their doctor than they needed and were selling the surplus at one pound per grain. (This was not because the doctors were behaving irresponsibly; it is very difficult to ascertain just how much an addict really does need.) Ultimately then all the heroin which was being 'pushed' in this way could be traced back to a prescription issued to someone. The Brain Report was therefore correct in saying that 'the major source of supply has been the activity of a very few doctors who have prescribed excessively for addicts'.

One of the best-known and most respected doctors who had been prescribing for addicts (known as 'junkies' doctors') was Dr. A. J. Hawes. He wrote to *The Observer* on September 12, 1965:

. . . the black market in these drugs is fed by over-prescribing doctors. I may be one of these myself, although I do my best not to be. There is no other source of supply beyond an occasional and negligible robbery of a chemist's shop. To cut off the supply by prescription would be easy; it has been done in the United States, where doctors are not allowed to prescribe for addicts, with the result that the provision of drugs has become a flourishing industry, and drug addiction there increases yearly. So we arrive at the curious anomaly that if we are to keep big business off the black market trade in drugs, we need a number of over-credulous, over-sympathetic, over-prescribing doctors, unless we want to run the serious risk of having thousands of addicts on our hands, instead of the few hundreds we have at present.

Dr. Hawes claimed that it was the presence of these G.P.s which kept the black market from expanding in Britain as it had done in the United States. But what has happened since the Brain Report? First, as we saw earlier, some of the small group of 'junkies' doctors' ceased prescribing for addicts, and the number of doctors willing to prescribe heroin on the National Health Service also dwindled. As a result the illicit traffic has increased. Further letters from Dr. Hawes show the change in the situation during 1966 and 1967. On November 15th, 1966, he wrote to *The Times*:

One of the prominent junkies' doctors' has just thrown up his addicts practice in the past few days. I cannot blame him but the result has been to throw about 80 heroin and cocaine addicts on the open market, which usually means the black market. In the past 48 hours I have had 10 new applicants for supplies, whom I have had to turn away from my door – most regretfully. . . . The most threatening portent is that addicts are telling me that there is plenty of the stuff to be had on the black market, even though the source from over-prescribing doctors is drying up. It looks as if big business which has been waiting in the wings for so long has now taken over the stage and is playing the lead.

On June 27th, 1967, he wrote further:

During the past few weeks I hear from my heroin addicts that the drug is now appearing on the black market in powder form, which has never been available before. Tablets have always been the form of the drug in this country. It looks as if my dismal prophecy of large-scale heroin merchants waiting their opportunity of a shortage in the black market which has been fed up to now by wicked over-prescribing 'junkie' doctors has come to fulfilment. The little plastic bag seems to be replacing the tablet, and as a powder is more easily adulterated than a tablet, the new regime is looked upon with disfavour by such addicts as I have asked. Unfortunately when, as in America, the big boys control the black market, then there will be no choice. Take the powder or leave it, and we all know what the addicts' choice will be. The next few months are going to be very interesting. The Ministry of Health does not seem to understand the implications of what they are doing. Nevertheless, they soon will.

It is very important to stress these dangers since we are often told that there is little danger of a black market in heroin developing in Britain. After the Brain Report, medical sources for heroin on the National Health Service began to dry up, and the official Report from the Home Office to the United Nations for 1965 expressed concern at the 'significant increase . . . in the number of addicts who have obtained their drugs entirely from unknown sources.' After April 1968, when only licensed doctors at clinics were allowed to prescribe heroin, the amount of heroin prescribed has gradually dropped with the substitution of methadone (Physeptone). It is since this time that a form of illicit powder heroin from Hong Kong ('Chinese heroin') has increased in circulation. Since this time also more addicts have started to 'fix' barbiturate and other non-opiate drugs. It is by no means clear whether the illicit traffic in injectible drugs will increase. If an organised criminal black market gets a hold in Britain, the consequences will be very grave indeed.

QUESTIONS FOR DISCUSSION

1. Why do you think people become heroin addicts? How would you advise a person who was attracted by heroin?

2. Is heroin itself dangerous, or is it the addict's personality which is the real danger?
3. Were doctors to blame for the increase in heroin addiction?
4. Has the restricting of prescribing of heroin been a good decision?
5. If heroin is so dangerous, why not ban it altogether?
6. Why is there little black market in heroin in Britain? Will this always be so?
7. Describe the differences between heroin addiction in Britain and the U.S.A.

5

SOCIAL CAUSES OF DRUG MISUSE

IN chapter 2 we outlined what addiction means, and the difference between addiction and dependence; and then in later chapters we have shown what particular problems are associated with drug-taking in Britain. In this chapter we will try to sort out why it is that some people take drugs and others do not, and we will look into the backgrounds of people who have become dependent on or addicted to drugs.

It is hardly surprising really that in a world of doubtful standards, where wrong and misery are all around us, people become reliant on drugs. The heads of government seem determined to destroy the world by their retention of nuclear and other weapons of man's destruction. War, instead of being looked upon with horror and every effort made to prevent and stop it, is commonplace. We see headlines of man's destructions in a 5-day war, and we forget the individual misery of the family, relatives and friends of each person killed or maimed. We throw away milk into disused mines when we have a surplus, forgetting that two thirds of the world's population is starving. We tend to think James Bond is marvellous, even though he destroys people all around him. Comics, magazines, paperbacks, television and films scream at us that life is cheap.

Is it any wonder that in such a society as ours, where destruction and contempt for human life abound, some people feel they have every right to destroy themselves, either by drinking too much, by driving their cars too fast, or by taking drugs? Addiction to hard drugs is a chronic form of suicide – a form of self-destruction, and it is not surprising that addicts choose destruction for themselves just as the world leaders glibly talk about war – which is a choice of destruction not only for themselves, but for all of us.

Most people who take hard drugs for the first time know the effects of the drugs. These are two-fold, however; although the drug enables them to escape the problems of feeling inadequate, the monotony of everyday life, and the inability to communicate, giving the feeling of well-being and 'highness', it also produces its own problem – that of tolerance (the building up of resistance in the body to the drug, so that more and more is needed to get the same effects) and addiction (as we saw in chapter 2). Very often the potential addict sees all too clearly the mess around him in his own life, the violence and destruction in society, which shows itself in everyday living, and, consciously or unconsciously, chooses self-destruction rather than take part in the society around him whose values disgust him.

On the other hand those who indulge in occasional pill-taking and cannabis-smoking tend to be young people who are without any particular direction or aim in life, who may well be utterly bored with their monotonous existence at home, at school, or at work. During our upbringing we have tended to be *taught* only, not educated, and so often we find extreme difficulty in sorting our lives out, establishing our own identities, and finding a particular purpose in life.

Under-stimulation or boredom with life in the suburbs, or too great an identification with pop and folk music stars and other teenage 'cult idols' causes discontent and frustration. Identification means that one person relates himself to another person until the first person sees himself as the other; an emotional tie, by which he behaves or imagines himself behaving as if he were the other person. We all

have these daydreams, but when we look at ourselves and
see we have not the talent the pop stars have, nor the
money to dress and behave as they do, we can get utterly
depressed. It sometimes seems so unfair when someone
of our own age gets to the top, becomes famous and leads
what seems such an exciting or mysterious life. How we
envy them! But we must remember that we only see the
glamorous side; we don't see the heartbreak of the long
struggle to the top. We don't see the long hours of practice,
the unhappiness in personal lives, the unglamorous nights
without sleep, long train journeys, bad publicity, no
privacy – all the things which go with fame. Our idols may
seem to have a fabulous life – having fun and spending
money – but do remember they also are human beings and
they are often feeling really unhappy or ill when they have
to appear to be so elated on stage. Often the life they lead,
without proper rest, sleep and relaxation causes them to
be constantly under a doctor's supervision and treatment.

Previous 'Teenage Rebellions'

After the second world war there was a steep rise in
juvenile delinquency. There was also a feeling of relaxation among parents who had been worried and miserable
and tensed up for the long years of the war. People began
to move back to the cities which were bombed and tried
to remake their lives. The children suffered, as they were
in a *conflict* situation. They did not understand the sudden
change from tension and death every day to the new kind
of relaxation; they did not understand that national enemies
of yesterday were now rapidly becoming friends of today.
They grew up with violence and aggression all around
them, and did not understand how and why the adults now
said it was wrong to kill, to fight, to break things. So the
young were very confused – added to which many of them
had moved around from town to country, country to town,

during the years of their childhood; from mother to foster mother and back to mother – and many had hardly seen their fathers during their years of growing up. All these factors caused a wave of aggression and behaviour against society in the years after the war ended in 1945, until well into the late 1950s. In America much the same thing happened, but large gangs formed, where the youngster could feel he belonged – even if he was terrified of his leader and fellow members.

Then a strange thing happened – during the late 1950s the confusion began to clear in the minds of many then young people and they began to rebel against authority, because they saw that political policies geared to destruction (for example nuclear bombs and chemical warfare weapons) were formulated by authority 'at the top'. It is natural for most children to rebel against their parents as they get older – for parents often stop them doing things they want to do; but this particular rebellion of teenagers and others was against society, against false values, against war and destruction, against waste and fighting; it wanted peace, brotherhood, food for all, freedom for all – in fact, a whole new social policy based on love, not hate. Many marched with CND (Campaign for Nuclear Disarmament) and committed civil disobedience with the Committee of 100 in the early 1960s. 'Juvenile delinquency' still went on, as it did after the end of the Second World War, but instead of the destruction and aggression vented in the earlier era, this generation wanted a constructive new social policy. The new rebellion was against authority being destructive (or *anti-social*, against society, as delinquency is supposed to be). It was against destruction, and for construction.

The older generation tried to stamp out the rebellion and equated it with depraved morals, loose living, 'no-goodness' and personal dirt. Just as today much of the bad publicity about drug-taking confuses drug-taking with complete moral depravity. Often drug-taking is made to seem very much worse than it is by the mixing up of hard and soft drugs in press coverage and talks –and by including cannabis (or 'pot') with heroin and cocaine. Alongside this perhaps deliberate confusion lies another; that of linking sex and drugs and trying to shock the world into stamping out 'drug-taking and its resulting dreadful sexual activities'. This is stupid, of course. Addicts to heroin, for example, are mostly incapable of any sexual activity; and cannabis is not an aphrodisiac (producing sexual desire). Many pill-takers find that these drugs suppress the sexual appetite, and are mostly taken in circumstances of private parties and all night club sessions, that is, in the company of many other people.

Today's 'Rebellion'

Just as drugs, long hair and pop music are associated and identified with the young, so allegations of their sexual depravity and promiscuity, their 'fallen morals' and an envisaged 'bad end' are associated with the established older generation – the weapons used against teenagers by their parents. There has always been this conflict between what are called proximate generations, and it seems to occur quite naturally in many countries and cultures all over the world. In some villages in some African tribes, one generation lives on one side of the village, and the parents on the other side. The grandparents in turn live on the opposite side to their own children (so that grandparents and grandchildren live on the same side). This way of separating the generations relieves the tensions in society and is called a system of 'alternate generations'. So it can be seen that this rebellion against authority symbolised by parents and their generation is not just confined to the British teenager – it can be seen all over the world, and is one way in which society progresses.

But it is a long step from mini skirts and records of the 'Stones' to being an addict to heroin and cocaine. So there must be something other than just these external causes which make a person become 'hooked' on drugs. These causes just mentioned set the scene, paint the backcloth only, and other individual internal forces within each of us ultimately decide what we do. The external factors or *environment*, are very important and in many aspects mould the internal factors, but ultimately the internal factors decide what we do, drawing on the experience we have gained from the environment. For example, if we had lived on a desert island all our lives we would not become addicts, because there would have been no drugs around in the environment; but if we had been rescued and put back into a civilization we might well turn then to whichever drugs existed in the new environment around us, seeking solace from the despair felt at coming back into such an awful place as 'civilization' – and might very well long to be back on the quiet, peaceful, desert island!

Internal Causes of Drug Misuse

One of the most striking reasons why people take drugs is that they want to change their mood or how they feel. Of course, it is not true that everyone who wants to change his mood takes drugs. For example, if you are made very angry by something or someone, you often feel you want to hit them or throw something – and the amazing thing is that if you do carry out your wishes your anger often just goes and you feel relieved and relaxed again. In this way you have effected a change of mood – from hot anger and tension to a feeling of relief and even a kind of shame at losing your temper or self-control. However, during the time of anger the body itself is effecting a chemical change by the release of adrenalin into the blood stream, which causes the heart to beat more quickly, the muscles to be more ready for action, and releases energy from the body's store, for intense and sustained activity.

We have seen in a medical setting how tranquillizers (or barbiturates) are used to prevent anxiety and produce sleep; how amphetamines ('pep pills') are used to stimulate very depressed people, or for slimming purposes; how the opiates (including heroin and morphine) are used to relieve extreme pain; how LSD has been used by a few psychiatrists to help mentally ill patients; and how alcohol and cannabis are used in different countries in a socially acceptable setting. We have also seen how drugs are misused outside the medical setting, and the consequences of misuse (dependence and addiction). Drugs are misused when they are applied without medical supervision, and the mind and body are misused by trying to change the character or mood with the application of drugs. It was mentioned above that when anger is vented, the mood changes. It is natural to be angry, to release energy and to feel less tense after such a release. If the anger is bottled up it makes us bad-tempered for a long time; and if we never show our feelings we store up the unspent energy until it either explodes or is channelled into another activity – beating the dog for example, or pulling the cat's tail. But over the years since you were a baby you have learned to control your temper up to a certain point. It would be an impossible world if we all started to scream, bang our heads, cry and throw things (as we did when a baby) every time anything angers us, or goes wrong in any way. For this reason, and because we learned to use language to explain what we wanted and to communicate with other people who could supply our needs, we learned to *control* this aggressiveness. We learned to change our character and our mood as we grew up in order to control our tempers.

Insecurity

However, certain parts of our personality are more diffi-cult to cope with. What do we do if we are always feeling lonely, depressed or shy? How do we change these un-pleasant moods? How do we stop feeling 'the odd one out' (*alienated*)? How can we stop feeling unsure of ourselves, thinking we have no confidence or that no-one likes us? The answers to these questions are many. With some people it is a question of finding out the answers for them-selves as they grow up; others find that parents or teachers can help; with others it is easier to get help from a priest or a youth-club leader; while others find these 'personality problems' can best be dealt with by help from a doctor or psychiatrist. Everyone goes through stages of feeling insecure, being uncertain of themselves and unsure of the world around them. As you grow up so many things which you just accepted as true when a child because your mother or teacher, for example, told you so, are seen in a different light. Often you see pure untruths were told you when you were smaller – and the obvious thing to do is to try and find out *why* you were told untruths (because it was probably only a system of 'white lies' either to protect you from something, or because it is sometimes extraordinarily difficult to explain adult concepts to young children). Cast your memory back to when you believed in Father Christmas – and then remember what happened to you when you found out that it was not true that he came down the chimney. In probably eight out of ten cases the child learns from his school friends that Father Christmas does not exist and when he challenges his parents with this new-found knowledge he may very well consider his parents lied to him, misled him or deliberately cheated him.

From this example it is easy to see how a tremendous amount of insecurity – or unsureness – is built up. Can you remember ever being lost as a child? Did you ever think your mother had left you for good (or perhaps you were one of those unfortunate ones whose mother or father did leave them or die)? Can you remember the absolute feeling of panic and despair? This again is called insecurity; you are unsure of your position, your family and your future – in a nutshell, you are unsure of yourself in relation to your family, home and school, that is, your entire environment. Many people go all through their lives being unsure of themselves and what they should do. Many such people find that this insecurity causes them to be very lonely and feel cut off from the rest of mankind. Many more are insecure with regard to family, friends, job and self-confidence. At parties they always feel left out of it, and are too shy to start a conversation with someone they don't know. Over the years, luckily, many people have learned to control their overwhelming feelings of insecurity (such as that experienced by the lost child) and the anxiety and tension which comes with it. Many more have been helped to overcome it with the help of a friend, doctor, social worker, psychologist, etc.

But what about those who do not learn to control their anger and other moods of their personality, and those who do not meet a person able to help them? Some become just very unhappy people; some become mentally ill; some become criminals or 'juvenile delinquents'; some become cynical and never see any good in anything without being sure that hidden away there is a bad bit waiting to take over the good, that soon the pleasure will be turned to hurt, that pain is always following joy. A few become dependent or addicted to drugs.

It is not true that *everyone* who ends up taking drugs without a doctor's advice to start doing so (i.e. without for example, taking barbiturates to help reduce their tension) feels insecure or can't control their moods. But it is true that *many* people who take drugs have just these problems.

The question arises, why do some people find no difficulty in solving their problems and yet others cannot even begin to do so? Why do some take refuge in drugs and alcohol and others do not? It depends on several factors. Firstly, if you are able to get help when you want it, then you can sort out your problems and fears. If you are not able to express your difficulties because you are afraid or shy, then the problems are probably increased. Secondly, one person may never feel lack of confidence, lonely, depressed, unloved, insecure, etc. while another may feel all these things. It may be that these are two different personality types; or it may be that one had more favourable circumstances in his upbringing and at home and school than the other. Thirdly, one person may be helped over his difficulties, while another has been laughed at (which does not help at all). Fourthly, one may have felt that adults do not practice what they preach, and have double standards, saying one thing and doing another, while another may never have been sensitive to this peculiarity of 'maturity' at all.

What evidence we have about young people who have become addicted to or dependent on drugs shows us that they have had difficulties and problems that they were not able to deal with, and they sought refuge from these problems in the dream world of drugs. There are the few exceptions to this rule. A few started to take drugs deliberately in order to become 'hooked' or a 'junkie'. Some of these did this because it provided a way in which they could 'get back' at their parents, teachers, society, etc. – by being what their elders call a failure or misfit. These, fortunately, are the few cases. Of course, it is natural to want some kind of revenge against authority, whether it is parents, teachers, priest, older brother or sister, society, etc. In some cases it is more than right, it is one's duty to kick against authority. For example, we must always be vigilant against tyranny, oppression, exploitation and badly administered authority. It is right to demonstrate one's dislike of people who abuse power given to them; and it is one's duty to prevent corruption in high places. The people who take drugs, however, in order to spite their parents, for example, are not only succeeding in this aim, but they are also succeeding in hurting themselves, even in poisoning their bodies with drugs; and they are, in fact, punishing themselves for not being what their parents expected them to be. You might call this self-infliction a form of masochism – hurting themselves for the pleasure of seeing how they hurt their parents.

Ignorance

A lot of people who begin to take drugs on their own do not actually know what they are doing. It is surprising how difficult it is for us to admit that we do not know what something is about – or to admit our ignorance of it. Many people started taking drugs in ignorance, not knowing what the drugs were or what they were supposed to do, or how many to take to get the desired effect, rather than admit that they did not know anything about the drugs and their effects. This is also a form of shyness and insecurity – not being able to face your friends when you are ignorant – an inability to let them see you are not so knowledgeable and daring about these things as they appear to be. The amazing thing is that if you *do* challenge their knowledge you will probably find *they* do not know either!

Social pressure

Another type of situation when people start taking drugs is under social pressure. This means that your friends, or your group, exert pressure on you in one way or another so that you conform to what the rest are doing or want. This happens in every group no matter what age, what country, or what they have in common which makes them a group. Because they are a group they have certain rules and expect certain behaviour from all who belong to it.

All groups expect conformity to what the group stands for. For example, conformity among members of a sailing club to the love of sailing and the rules of the rivers and seas; conformity of members of a coffee/social club to love of dancing and music; conformity of Members of Parliament to Parliamentary procedure and etiquette. If some member or members do not agree with the others or are always being different or awkward, then the others ask them to either change their attitude or leave, because they are upsetting the rest of the group and its cohesion or 'togetherness'. This phenomenon is called *social pressure* from the rest of the group on the *deviant* to conform. A deviant is the one who is not conforming to what the rest of the group wants. It depends on how strongly the deviant wants to stay with the group whether he leaves or changes his attitude when asked to do so.

Another form of social pressure exists – that of having to keep up with the rest for fear of losing face by, for example, being called 'chicken'. Many people were first introduced to drug-taking for this very reason. It certainly takes great courage to run the risk of being excluded from the group by being called 'chicken'. It takes even more courage to admit ignorance as well. But it is easy to see how teenagers conform to the rest of the group over drug misuse. If the individual wants to keep going with the group, and the group takes pills, or smokes 'pot', the individual often gives in to the majority even though it may be against his personal scruples.

Much has been written about the problems of teenagers today. It is true, though, that teenagers, both boys and girls, are continually under social and commercial pressure, through advertising, to keep up-to-date with fashion, hair styles, dances, records, etc., and a particular type of insecurity is felt by the young person who is not really attractive, has little money (who, for example, is still at school and whose friends are out at work) or who is not a good social mixer. The competition facing both sexes is very complex and, during the process of keeping one's status and position among one's friends and contemporaries, the teenager can be very unhappy and feel very inadequate. Often these difficulties contribute to child/parental relationships breaking down, and the teenager feels he is swimming right in the middle of a great pool, with no shoreline. Very many young mothers and wives often feel they can't cope with home, children, husband, work and shortage of money, and they turn to reliance on drugs to solve their problems. So it is not entirely a teenage problem!

In Summary

What have we said so far about the causes of addiction? We have shown that it is sometimes more difficult for one person to control his personality features than it is for another; that one person may suffer from feelings of insecurity, while another may not; that one person may be able to cope with his problems while another may not; that we may well be trying to identify with those we admire; how some people start drug taking to spite their parents or other people in authority; and finally, how it is often ignorance or social pressure which causes drug taking to commence, particularly among younger people.

As we saw in the first part of this chapter it seems to

be people with particular problems who become addicted to or dependent on drugs. The potential addict, for example, is almost certainly a person who feels insecure, unloved, alone, unhappy with himself or life. He is very sensitive, and prefers to take heroin as a refuge from these problems by opting out of society, instead of realizing that he is creating other problems by his addiction. He may not know that there are people available to help him cope with his problems and overcome them – or, at least, learn to live with them. He may very well reject such help.

Some housewives do become very depressed at times, and can't stand the pace of things. They find their existence intolerable when they remember the happy times before marriage – or what they thought were happy times. Often a doctor gives them tablets or pills to help them get over their troublesome and anxious times. Some need psychiatric help in order to learn to live with their problems and to prevent them causing more tension by worrying about them. Likewise some teenagers become very troubled with school work, relations at home, boy/girl friend troubles, feelings of loneliness, sexual problems, fears of meeting new people, and so on. Those who are wise talk to someone who can help them with their problems; others put them aside by shielding themselves from them – by taking drugs to enable them to forget; to make their mood change for the better or worse; to make them lively enough to stay awake at the week-ends; or to enable them to have self-confidence or make conversation and face other people.

The question may arise now that if it is all right to take drugs when prescribed them by a doctor, why is it not so to take them without a doctor? The answer is very simple, and in two parts. First, we know by now it is dangerous to take drugs without a doctor's recommendation to do so, because we do not, ourselves, understand all the intricacies of drugs and their side effects, and the doctors do, and because some drugs lead to addiction and some to dependence. Second, there are many thousands of different types of drugs. In the pill and capsule variety often as many as 30 look exactly the same size and colour. It is only an expert pharmacologist, with special measuring equipment, who can tell which drug a particular pill is. We have learnt that many pills are available on the 'black market' from supplies obtained by thefts from chemists, warehouses and wholesalers. When you buy a pill on the 'black market' you have absolutely no guarantee that the pill is what it is supposed to be. The 'pusher' is not a pharmacist and cannot by eye distinguish one of thirty different types of drug which the pill could be – so he cannot really know if the pill is Drinamyl or not. He probably took them on trust from the person who stole them, and there is no guarantee that the right pills were stolen. One example of such a situation occurred in Birmingham, when teenagers bought blue pills on the 'black market' as 'blues' and they later were found to be aspirin dipped in blue ink!

So the point here is that, apart from dangers of becoming dependent on pills, there is no guarantee that the pills you think you are taking as 'blues' or 'bombers' are in fact these pills.

QUESTIONS FOR DISCUSSION

1. What would you say are the reasons people start using soft drugs?
2. Are these reasons the same for people who become addicted to heroin?
3. Why do teenagers rebel against their parents? Is this a good thing?
4. Teenagers and other people actively rebel against

authority. Is this rebellion justified or is it to be condemned?

5. What are 'personality problems' and how are these related to drug taking?

6. What makes a person feel insecure and how does this affect his life?

7. Do people start taking drugs through ignorance?

8. What is meant by social pressure and what has this to do with drug misuse?

9. If it is considered right to take drugs when prescribed by your doctor, then why is it not right to take the same drugs when they are offered on the 'black market'?

6

SIGNALS AND DANGER SIGNS

Prevention

THERE is an old and very true saying that 'prevention is better than cure'. Prevention means doing something about a difficulty before it becomes a problem. In medicine it means taking precautions or inoculation against contracting a disease. As a young child you were probably given *vaccinations* against smallpox and poliomyelitis and *inoculations* against diphtheria and tuberculosis. This is preventive medicine, ensuring that you will not suffer from a disease, by taking steps to prevent your having it. It is very much cheaper and better to prevent disease than to try and treat it after it has been contracted, because often unpleasant side effects arise alongside the main illness. For example, weakening of the eyesight or even blindness, can accompany the common disease of measles. It is better, therefore, to prevent the person getting measles and so avoid the risk of being blind than to treat him after he has contracted measles. It is particularly relevant in mental illness because unlike, say, chickenpox which is over and done with in a few weeks, mental illness takes much longer to cure. So it is of utmost importance to prevent mental illness and one way of doing this is to deal with difficulties before they become burdensome problems.

Knowledge is a very good inoculation against things going wrong, especially against fear and confusion. As babies we thought that mother had gone forever every time she went out of the room, and we cried loudly in protest and fear at being left alone. As we grew a little older we gained the knowledge that mother came back again – and this prevented our fear when she left the room. As young children we all probably experienced fear of the dark, but when we could manage to turn on the light we lost our fear of the dark, as we could ourselves change the situation and turn dark into light if we felt afraid. Thus the ability to turn on the light *inoculated* us against fear of the dark.

You may well have experienced a situation where you were confused through ignorance – like going into a geography examination and not knowing anything about the area to be tested; or having a science test sprung on you and not having time to look up formulae and methods. In another setting you may well have been confused at the dinner table in a good restaurant because you did not know what all the cutlery was for. In each of these situations, knowledge beforehand of what was coming, experience or teaching on how to deal with any problem arising, would have saved fear, worry, confusion and unhappiness.

Much emphasis is laid nowadays on the need for sex education as well as academic education. It is not only sex education which is needed but a complete *social* education. The idea behind sex education is that ignorance leads to unhappiness and probably unwanted children, and education teaches us the facts about sex, in particular the biological facts and what the results are of combinations of sexual germ cells. Unfortunately, much teaching of this kind on the subject of sex does not have its desired effect. What should be taught are the answers to *your* questions. Moral teaching apart, and there is a great value in the teaching of the right morals here (for example, the differences between love, sex and lust), there are many fundamental questions on sex which you never get a chance to ask an older person about. Getting the answers to your questions helps to inoculate you against frustration, fear, unhappiness and anxiety on the subject of sex.

This is exactly what we mean by inoculation; and the medical analogy supports this. Once inoculated and armed with the facts against ignorance, we are *preventing* the dangerous results from actions we know little or nothing about. There are, however, as with the causes of drug-taking and its misuse, two types of prevention – one connected with external circumstances and the other with internal circumstances.

External factors of prevention

Of course, if drugs were not available on the 'black market', then you would not be in danger of buying them. If the papers and other publicity had not brought drugs to your attention you may never have heard of the 'drug problem'. Some people will even say that you should not be given lectures on drugs or be allowed to read books like this.

The first two observations are right in themselves of course, but, unfortunately, both situations exist and so one has to accept them and learn to live with them – making up your own mind on the issues which arise. You can gain help from teachers, parents, priests, doctors and from this book, we hope – to enable you to sort out the fact from the fiction about drugs – to enable you to make a balanced judgement, with help from others when needed.

Those who think you should not be told about drugs argue that if you are shielded from knowledge of the exist-ence of drugs, then you will not be enticed into taking them. The argument is based on two contentions: (a) that talking about drugs may make you want to experiment with them out of curiosity and so bring you to going out to look for illegal drugs and possibly bring you into bad company, and (b) that if you do not know the problem exists, there is no point in drawing it to your attention. Others believe there is greater danger in ignorance about the existing misuse of drugs, because sooner or later you may well be confronted with people taking drugs illegally, and you will be better protected against any danger by knowing the truth. If you can't make up your mind about drugs, you can intelligently discuss the subject with older people once you know the facts.

Having read the last chapter you may very well say that it is society's fault that the world is such a bad and rotten place to live in – its standards are all wrong and it doesn't practice what it preaches. We may agree with you, but remember that there are good things as well as bad in the world and in society. If you look for it you can always find the good as well as the bad; and remember that every one of us *is* society. Maybe today it is your parents' generation which is in a position of authority and you may blame them for all the mess we are in; but tomorrow – in a few years – your age group will be in control of society, its standards and morals. You will probably be the parents of rebellious children, and you will be the legislators and the teachers. What kind of mess or success you make of society will be up to you. But from today you can start the prevention process – the prevention of any 'disease' in society in ten or twenty years' time.

The answer to changing society lies in really reforming it and this involves the positive challenging of authority. If you challenge you must have reasons for doing so, and you must be ready to put forward positive alternatives and suggestions. The challenging of society is often accompanied by an ignorance of how things are run. Learning how things happen and why they exist is an excellent way of finding out how to change things for the better. It is also an excellent form of preventing the same wrong things happening again in the future.

Internal factors of prevention

Most people feel very mixed up and confused as they grow up. Both internal and external factors combine to produce these feelings. If you remember what we said in the last chapter you will know that background environment is an important factor in the behaviour of those who misuse drugs. As children we learned certain standards and morals in school, at home, in church, in clubs, and then as we grew older we found that the people who preached at us did not practise what they preached, but still expected us to practise it. Later we found, perhaps, that two sets of standards exist in the world; the ideal ones, set out on paper and taught to children, and the actual ones – those which really happened. We learned as children that it was wrong to lie, to steal, to hate, to hurt, and as we grew up we saw around us a world which allowed men to kill other men, to maim women and children with napalm bombs, to hate men because of the colour of their skins, to lie to protect property and money, and to steal and cheat as much as possible from 'authority'. Evasion of taxes, stealing or wasting work-time, clocking in the wrong hours on the time-sheets are all apparently 'accepted'. The world about us seems to adopt another set of standards to those we were supposed to uphold; and understandably, there is confusion in the minds of many young people, together with a sense of frustration because they can see no way of changing the way the world is run. It is hardly surprising that one gets so depressed!

However, we can't just give up. We have to learn to live with society, otherwise we would all be in a mental hospital with nervous breakdowns.

Learning to live with society around us by no means suggests *accepting* society for what it is, for this would mean succumbing to what we find wrong in it. Learning to live with society around us means that (a) we know what is wrong with that society, (b) we know what we want it to be like and (c) we will try to alter society for the better – starting with ourselves and our relations and dealings with other people.

Attitudes

Often we have an attitude towards something in our environment, which, in turn, affects our behaviour. For example, we may have an attitude towards people from the West Indies, which could make us either very 'pro' or 'anti' West Indians in general. Often we have no direct experience of them but have assumed an attitude towards them from other people, our parents, Press reports, stories and gossip. Once we actually meet a number of West Indians ourselves it is more than likely that our attitude changes. For instance, we may find that we like them very much, whereas before we were afraid of them. In this way, knowledge has changed the attitude for the better. In this case we have learned to behave in a more positive way towards West Indians.

Attitudes may serve to protect us from an unpleasant truth about ourselves. For example, a person who feels very insecure himself may develop a hostile attitude (or prejudice in this case) against minority groups (such as the West Indians in Britain) so that he himself can feel superior. In this way he hides from himself his real feeling of insecurity. The bully usually fits into this category; he persecutes weaker people so that he may feel superior. but, in fact, he is often, himself, a weak and cowardly person. This form of disguising one's bad points and failures can be seen in drug-taking, too. An addict is hardly ever a bully or violent person, however, although he does seem to persecute *himself* by his addiction.

The point we want to make here is that if a person feels himself behaving in a way which is really different from his own beliefs, it is often easier to change the behaviour than to change the belief. If he finds he is tempted to take drugs without a doctor telling him to do so, he may well be going against his own strongly held beliefs, and he will find it easier to change his behaviour rather than his beliefs. If he has an attitude to drugs which is based only on what other people have told him, and he feels it must be 'fabulous' to take drugs, then he should find out more facts, because he *may* find the facts don't fit the image given by word of mouth, and he might want to change his attitude towards drugs!

Alienation

Alienation means being or feeling you are on your own, alone, outside the group. Some people feel alienated and unattached all their lives, but it is a phenomenon which can be closely associated with the maturation process. In many ways it is frustrating and frightening to 'grow up'. Suddenly you are faced with the world, and being thought of as a person in your own right. Suddenly the whole social life extends before you – with its clothes, records, make-up, cars, clubs. Suddenly you may realize you are not part of this gaiety. Perhaps you have not as much money as the rest; perhaps you don't mix well and are shy, or even terrified of the opposite sex – or even the same sex! Perhaps you can't face the competition from others.

You may be the odd man out. You may prefer Bach and Beethoven to the Beatles and The Who; you may prefer books to dancing; your own company to that of others. You may feel you have a special task in life and don't know how to set about it; you may well be worried because you can't think what to 'be' when you leave school. You may even want to opt out completely and 'be' nothing but just yourself 'on the road'.

Or you may be so confused all round that all you want to do is forget it all. It is precisely such a state of confusion which has led some young people to start taking to drugs, in the hope that these will solve their problems (at least until tomorrow). But neither the taking of drugs, nor wanting to forget it all will do any good. The only answer is to prevent this state of affairs happening.

Whenever you have a problem you can't cope with, whether it's school work, parent problems, spots, overweight, shyness, boy/girl friend trouble, etc., there is always someone who can and will give you help. Many of those available are trained and paid to help you; so give them the chance to use their experience to your advantage. It is so much better to 'get it off your chest' than to keep a problem all bottled up inside until you are so tense that you *have* to see a doctor.

Don't be afraid to ask, even what may seem simple or impossible questions, for example, 'Why do I argue with my parents?' 'How "far" can I go with "necking"?' 'Can I live away from home and still go to school?' 'How can I stop blushing?' Behind all these questions, and other apparently simple ones, are a multitude of complexities which the trained person can help you sort out and understand. Don't be ashamed or afraid of asking for this particular kind of help. You might well be surprised to know how many people, much older than you, are often very mixed up and unsure over something which may seem quite simple to you! They need help when they can't 'see the wood for the trees' – we all do; and there is always someone to guide us through the forest into a clearing where we can see the difficulties around us and how to approach them from a new angle.

On the other hand it is not true that there is a quick and easy way of solving all problems. It may take time and effort, but it takes no more time sorting them out than worrying about them and allowing them to get bigger and even more difficult to solve. People who can help, in their different ways are: parents, teachers, doctors, psychologists, social workers, youth leaders, priests, probation officers, Citizens' Advice Bureaux, health visitors, child guidance officers (in the Local Council).*

It is so much better to find out what the problem is all about, and get help with it, than to try to forget about it by taking drugs without medical advice. So many new problems arise when one starts taking drugs – and they are added to those already there! So you are worse off in the long run. It is good to remember that a man grows out of some problems with time and maturing – other problems grow with him. The best method of dealing with all of them is to prevent them getting bigger and unmanageable. And the best way to deal with the temptation to take drugs is to prevent it by being inoculated against ignorance of the effects of drugs and by preventing the mind getting to such a state that all it wants to do is to forget all its problems by any means whatsoever. In its advanced state it has been known that this kind of acute difficulty has sent some people into the position where they actually stole, tried to commit suicide, or set fire to places, in order to receive help in a hospital, mental hospital, or prison, because they were not able in some way or another to ask for help and receive it.

But, if a person already takes drugs and has accumulated problems it is not too late. He can still seek help and find out why he has to take drugs; and then he can be helped with his problem, as we shall see in the next chapter.

* If you have a problem and can't find someone to help you or are too embarrassed or shy to discuss it, you can write to the authors c/o Pergamon Press, Headington Hill Hall, Oxford, and they will try to put you in touch with the right person who can help with your problem.

What harm is there in taking pills?

You may disagree with all this and say that you can't see anything wrong in taking a few 'pep pills' to keep awake all week-end at parties or clubs. There *is* very little wrong in it, except that you will find you are breaking the law by the illegal possession of the drugs – that is, having them without being able to prove that you are taking them because a doctor prescribed them for you. You are liable to imprisonment and/or a fine. Medically, there is little harm in taking the occasional 'pep pill' or sleeping tablet. The danger lies in habitually taking them, becoming dependent on them, taking too many of them, mixing different pills during a weekend, and perhaps taking the wrong ones. Apart from the immediate dangers in taking these pills, the effects can be long term and, although it may seem crazy to think of it now, the effects may well not be felt for some 10 years or so. Lack of sleep and overworking the body-cells tells in early ageing and proneness to disease, particularly disease of the heart and circulation.

Prevention of escalation from 'soft' to 'hard' drugs

How can you avoid going on to heroin if you take pills and smoke 'pot'? First, you can stop and think, and see if you really want to become addicted to a suicidal drug, and whether you know exactly what you are doing. Secondly you can remove yourself from the society where you are likely to come into contact with people selling and using narcotics such as heroin and morphine. Thirdly, you can inform the owner of the establishment that you *think* such drugs are being 'pushed' on the premises. Fourthly, you can refuse to become involved, if you wish to stay with the same people.

There are a few people who are afraid because, in spite of trying to be otherwise, they are attracted to the 'junkie' way of life (or death) and are more than fascinated by the use of a needle and the effects of heroin. A few others feel that the only way in which they can really get back at their parents or society is by becoming a 'junkie'. Luckily there are many qualified people who can help those who have these feelings. Often talking about such a problem with a school nurse, matron, teacher, priest or doctor, can help to work it out.

In summary

We have told you the reasons why some people may want to start taking unprescribed drugs; and how to prevent problems becoming too large to handle. We have seen how drugs are sometimes taken to give the impression that the person is experiencing a happy, joyful life, while in fact they are covering up an aching inner loneliness. We have discussed why it is easier for us to prevent ourselves getting to the state where we rely on drugs to live than it is to cure dependence and addiction. This is what is meant by prevention being better than cure – because even after cure undesirable side effects can be left by disease. In the next chapter we will look into the possibilities of treatment and cure for those who have not been able to prevent drugs taking over their lives.

QUESTIONS FOR DISCUSSION

1. Why is prevention better than cure?
2. Is it possible to talk about our problems? If so, whom can we talk to? If not, why not?
3. Does it help solve problems if we talk about them and seek assistance?
4. Why are some people all 'confused' and 'mixed-up'? What can they do to ease this particular difficulty?
5. Would it be a good idea for children to be taught from a very early age to seek guidance on their personal

problems? If so, would this be effected through a 'problem corner' in schools, where children could seek advice?

6. Does it do any harm to discuss drug misuse?

7

TREATMENT AND CURE FOR
DRUG ADDICTION

The meaning of 'treatment' and 'cure'

WE know enough now to realize that drug-taking and addiction are not simple illnesses which can be 'cured', just as whooping cough or measles can be cured. Often drug-taking is an extremely involved problem, and to understand it we need to understand the whole personality of the individual drug-taker. We cannot 'treat' or 'cure' without the fullest understanding. So we have to be very careful about the use of terms. It is certainly possible to *treat* a patient for drug addiction, and the actual physical addiction can be *cured*. But psychiatrists understand that this alone does not mean that the addict is really cured, because merely removing the physical symptoms is not enough. Deep down, the addict still wants his drug; he is still psychologically dependent on it. So we can treat and cure addiction in its purely physical sense without treating or curing the addicted patient *as a person*, and so long as the root causes of addiction remain, no amount of hospital treatment will help. We need to remember that, while hospital treatment is important, the really fundamental cure for addiction lies in the complete healing of the personality.

Prevention and treatment

This is why, as we saw in the last chapter, prevention is so much better than treatment. It is better to prevent oneself from becoming addicted than to try to cure oneself afterwards. Prevention also means getting to know and understand our personality, finding out what our problems are, learning about the kinds of problems which have led others to misuse drugs, and learning how to deal and live with our problems. So prevention is itself a form of treatment, but it means treating ourselves as persons, and not treating 'drug addiction' as a separate problem. Remember that a teenager's drug-taking is often only the expression, one expression among many perhaps, of problems which lie beneath the surface. By uncovering these problems and facing them, we cut at the root of the need to misuse drugs.

Doctors, psychiatrists, psychologists, and other trained people have special experience in helping us to face our own problems. By co-operating with them we can prevent our problems becoming bigger and harder to solve. We also make ourselves healthier and happier because we aren't hiding from ourselves any more. Drug-taking is often a way of escaping from reality. The best treatment is to face up to the reality of ourselves and our shortcomings, the reality of the world and its shortcomings, and to begin to understand ourselves as people. By doing so we come to understand other people and their problems, too.

Can addiction be cured?

But what about a person who has become addicted, say, to heroin? Is there any hope of cure? Some doctors would say, 'No'; and we have to admit that there are many facts to support them. The relapse rate for heroin addicts after going through hospital cures is very high indeed. One doctor who has had three hundred heroin addicts as patients says that in only a few cases can he claim that an addict has kicked the habit. This is a depressing prospect. No one has yet found *the* cure for addiction to heroin, as they have for leprosy, for instance. Much medical research has to be done and this takes a very long time, for you can't use 'trial and error' methods in medicine because you are dealing with human beings' lives.

For the user of amphetamines the prospects are brighter. Many people, particularly teenagers, pass through the stages of experimenting with pills quite happily. But we must not get slap-happy about this. Some do become heavily dependent on large quantities of pep pills, and this can be as serious and as dangerous as, sometimes even more than, heroin. This happens when the drug-taker becomes mentally ill with the condition clinically known as 'psychosis'.

There are, of course, some sensational cures for addiction, but they are exceptional. The fact is that many addicts of hard drugs seem to be suffering from a serious personality disorder, and some are incurable. They will need a regular supply of drugs in order to live and function properly. A good many heroin addicts do not want to be cured and, without a dramatic reorganization of themselves as people, are incapable of being cured. They are enslaved to heroin, which is slowly killing them, and their actual death is only a matter of time. Heroin addiction is chronic suicide.

However, a few doctors and psychiatrists have devoted themselves to helping and treating addicts, but the process is long and hard for both doctor and patient. The work is still in the early experimental stages because, as said above, there is no one wonder cure for addiction.

Treatment facilities

What possibilities are there of getting treated for addiction? What kind of places exist for attempting to cure addiction? What, in fact, do we mean by 'treatment'? Sometimes, we mean admission to a hospital unit which specializes in addiction. Or we may mean an out-patient centre which *maintains* the addict at a certain dosage of his drug, and tries to help him. There is not one type of 'treatment centre' which can simply be set up by an authority. In the following pages we shall discuss some types of treatment which have been tried and are going on now.

When we talk of 'treatment centres' we have to allow for the fact that a good many addicts will need to be maintained with supplies of drugs permanently. They will need not so much treatment centres as 'maintenance centres'. But clearly not all addicts fit into this category, and medical treatment for addiction is possible. There are already a number of hospitals in London and elsewhere which accept addicts as in-patients. But there are not enough, and those which exist are often old-fashioned mental hospitals to which addicts are reluctant to go, even if they can get in, as no hospital keeps a lot of beds free, and often you have to wait for a long time, for instance, even to have your tonsils out. Again, they will go through the formal 'withdrawal process' (which means gradually weaning them from their drug, first by substituting other drugs, and finally cutting off the supply altogether), and soon afterwards be discharged. Without any effective after-care, they are soon back with their addict friends, or can't face the world alone, and are often 'hooked' again within twenty-four hours.

It is very important to stress that the present treatment facilities for drug addicts in hospitals are very bad indeed. But there are some good centres, where addicts can be helped to come off and re-adjust to a fuller and happy life. Also there are a number of out-patients clinics where teenagers who are addicted or just experimenting with drugs can receive help. Since 1968, more out-patient units have been established, and more in-patient addiction units are being opened.

The first stage for an addict seeking treatment is usually to register with an out-patient clinic. This means a clinic attached to a hospital and staffed by psychiatrists, social workers and nurses. Some clinics have day centres where the addict can spend a good deal of time. At the clinic he will probably be taken off heroin and put on methadone (Physeptone), and this will involve also getting him off the needle and on to an oral drug. In the United States, the method of treatment called 'methadone maintenance' has become very popular, and enables addicts to work and function effectively on methadone, a long-acting drug which controls the withdrawal symptoms from heroin. For some addicts, the final aim is total abstinence, but for others it is more a question of control of their drug use.

If an addict wishes to come off all drugs, he will probably be admitted into an in-patient unit (although some addicts come off on an out-patient basis). Here there will probably be group therapy and other forms of psychological and social help. But what happens when he is discharged from hospital? It is at this point that the danger of relapse is very great. A long period of after-care is necessary, and there are a number of centres where small groups of ex-users can stay for long periods. Some of these are Christian in their basis, such as the Coke Hole in Andover, or Life for the World in Gloucestershire, or the New Life Centre in Bromley. Others are organized by ex-addicts on a 'self-help' basis, like Synanon in the United States, or the Phoenix Houses. Some former addicts have joined communes or other types of community, and have found these to be effective non-drug treatment programmes.

The American situation

The situation is very different in the United States both regarding the relationship of addict to doctor and the form of treatment available. No doctor is allowed to prescribe narcotic drugs to an addict. It is against the law. But there are many thousands of persons addicted to the narcotic or hard drugs. They obtain drugs entirely on the 'black market' or by tricking a doctor into thinking they have a serious disease needing pain-killing treatment or by some other form of illegal activity. They are always, therefore, in danger of being arrested by the police and put forcibly into prison or hospital for treatment. Whether the addict goes direct to prison or for an enforced 'cure' in hospital makes a great difference to him in one respect, because in prison he has to go through the agonies of taking a 'cold turkey'. This is the process of direct withdrawal from the drugs he is addicted to, without being gradually weaned from them, and without the help of substitute drugs. The name 'cold turkey' is given to this process because during the agonies of withdrawal from the drug the addict has, among other withdrawal symptoms, violent attacks of hot and cold sweats and 'goose-flesh' – hence his flesh looks, especially as he is extremely pale, like a cold pre-packed turkey!

An American consultant, Kolb, says that 'sudden withdrawal, the so-called "cold turkey" treatment, is inhuman, dangerous and especially undermining to persons who are already burdened and handicapped by psychological afflictions. In former years, many addicts in prisons and public hospitals were forced to undergo this inhumanity from their keepers'. We, in Britain, think this treatment of patients is inhuman and unnecessarily brutal, and we condemn the American attitude of treating addicts purely as criminals in the first place. We, in Britain, say that addicts are sick people and need proper medical and psychiatric help. We do not put people in prison *because* they are addicts, as happens in America. The law in this country says that if a person obtains his drugs on prescription from a doctor or psychiatrist, then he is a sick person.

If he obtains drugs illegally then he has committed a crime and is liable to punishment as a criminal. The advantage of this system is that if a person gets himself addicted to, say, heroin, he can find help and obtain drugs legally while he is being given help. In America there is only one way of getting drugs (outside of those used as substitutes in hospitals during a 'cure', such as methadone) and that is by entering into criminal activity.

Because drugs are obtainable from responsible medical sources in Britain, we are very harsh on people who obtain drugs illegally and are, rightly, much more harsh on people who sell or 'push' illegally obtained drugs. In America, where all illegally obtained drugs must be bought from 'pushers', the addict very often has to steal and engage in other anti-social and criminal activity in order to 'support his habit' or get enough money to buy his drugs.

We, in Britain, have a much smaller percentage of people addicted to narcotics than America has. It is undoubtedly the fact that an addict can go to a doctor and get help, instead of being handed over to the law courts, that has made the British situation preferable to the American, and has kept the addict population in this country relatively low. We saw how it is necessary to cure both the physical and the psychological addiction if we are to attempt to make an addict well again; and this, of course, can never be achieved in prison, with present facilities.

When addicts are sent for enforced 'cures' in American hospitals, like Lexington in Kentucky, the relapse rate is very high. This means that after leaving the hospital, the patient returns to drugs, in most cases, very quickly. Many reasons are put forward for this phenomenon, but the most striking reason is that unless the addict really and truly wants to give up his habit of drugs, unless he can actually see the point of giving them up and can face life without them once more, then he will always go back on them as soon as he leaves the Government institution. No amount of forcing an addict to 'cures' and 'cold turkey' treatment will make him better, until he really and honestly decides he must do and can do without the drug himself. Often, in enforced 'cures', the addict goes through such acute agony with the withdrawal pain and the inhuman treatment while he is in the institution that he is only living for the day he can get out and have his first 'fix' in order to forget all the pain and horror of his 'cure'.

There is very little or no follow-up in America when a patient is discharged from hospital, and Kolb says, 'In some cities they are more likely to receive the attention of a policeman bent on finding whether they can be induced to use drugs again, than by a social worker or nurse who is anxious to guide them into socially useful activities and to strengthen their resistance to drugs. . . . Ideally, there should be a follow-up team of social workers and nurses who should confer with local agencies to find work, favourable environments and psychotherapy for discharged voluntary patients and paroled prison patients'.

This brief outline of the American system of treating addicts may well convince us that prison, compulsory hospitalization and 'cold-turkey' methods are not good ways to treat addiction. But it suggests another question, too. Is hospital treatment (of any kind) enough?

Is hospital treatment enough?

For various reasons, the relapse rate among addicts who have left hospital is very high. Clearly, much of the work of treating the causes of addiction must be done outside hospitals. Small research centres where drug-takers can receive help and where experts can study the social as well as the medical effects of drugs are important. One such centre in this country is called CURE and is situated in Chelsea. It is run by a group of doctors and other workers.

It sets out to understand the addict, to help him to understand his addiction and to offer full community care to him during his treatment, and during the long process of rehabilitation (restoring to a healthy and fulfilling life). There is a great need for similar centres in the districts where drug-taking is common. Hospitals can easily become isolated and remote from the social problems of the young drug-taker. One of the main reasons why there is such a high relapse rate is that many hospitals make no real contact with the addict's family and friends, and there is no proper after-care. Drug-taking is regarded simply as a medical problem. This is worse than useless. It is probably because of their close links with the communities in which they are situated that All Saints Hospital in Birmingham or St. Clement's Hospital in East London are more successful than most.

Again, while there are treatment facilities for heroin addicts and those who have been taking very large quantities of amphetamines (pep pills like 'black bombers' and 'blues'), there is not much help being given in hospitals to young people who have been trying to solve their problems by taking pills, but have not become dependent on them. Yet there are thousands of teenagers in this position, who take 'blues' at weekends, and may experience 'the horrors' after a weekend session in the clubs, but cannot really be regarded as 'addicts'. What kind of help can be given to them? The people who can help here are often youth leaders, who can discuss problems with the teenagers in their area, and can bring in, if required, a psychiatrist to help with particular problems. This is done in various cafés and clubs in and around central London, which serve as a base for people to resolve their difficulties and can achieve more than visits to a rather forbidding clinic could do.

The need for new approaches

But new approaches and methods need to be developed, and we can learn a lot from the United States here. For example, there is a very interesting group called *Synanon*, founded in 1958 by a former member of Alcoholics Anonymous. This is a community in which addicts and ex-addicts help each other. Any addict who wants to join must withdraw by 'cold turkey', that is without the help of other drugs. Then he must live in the community for at least two years. During this period there are meetings of groups of between eight and twelve for an hour and a half, three times each week. In these groups there is very free and often violent criticism by the members of each other. Members of Synanon work and have a small amount of pocket money.

From Synanon has developed another community, *Daytop Village*, in Staten Island, New York City. 'Daytop' stands for 'Drug Addicts Treated On Probation', and the community has above 90 ex-addicts. Daytop makes very little use of medical or psychological help, and its rules are very strict. For instance, at first, members cannot leave the house, or write letters, or have visitors. The important feature about Synanon and Daytop is that it is ex-addicts who are helping addicts, and there is a very strong sense of community.

Also in the United States there are advice and help centres in the problem districts of cities where addicts can get help.

In San Francisco, the Haight-Ashbury Free Clinic, set up at the height of the hippy explosion of 1967, offers a wide range of health care services for the young people in that area, and there are free clinics in many parts of the United States. There are also many all-night telephone services and crisis centres, drop-in centres, and so on. None of these methods can, of course, be simply transplanted and applied to Britain, but there has been, in the last few years, a growth in 24-hour telephone advice services on the lines of Release and BIT in London, and many of these advertise in the Underground press.

Drugs are a symptom

We have stressed repeatedly that the real problems are not drugs; they are only a symptom. We need to get beyond the mere drug-taking to the problems underneath. Of course, when the drug has got control of a person, when things have got to such a state that his body really needs drugs and cannot function without them – then hospital treatment is necessary. But even then, it is no use thinking that hospitalization can solve his problems. If he doesn't get beneath the surface, then he is really still addicted. And before this stage is reached, there is so much more that can be done. This is why most of the spade-work in sorting out drug problems is best done in out-patient clinics, or in coffee bars and youth clubs, where trained people can help to sort out the difficulties which can lead to drug addiction.

The 'group therapy' which is used in hospitals is also used in out-patient clinics. These are places to which people with problems (not only drug problems) can go, without payment, once a week, and discuss their problems with other people in a similar position. A psychiatrist is present at the group, but it is realized that while he can help a lot, ultimately the solution to a person's problems lies in himself. Information about group therapy can be obtained from mental health officers, probation officers, clergy or teachers. Most towns have clinics which run regular groups for young people, and they are very valuable ways in which we can learn to understand ourselves.

Getting to the root of the problem

'Getting to the root of the problem' means finding out

what makes us what we are. We face our personalities and see things which we didn't realize were there. Thus an individual may come to see why he took drugs, what his *motives* were. This is far more valuable than just relying on a few weeks in a hospital. A good doctor can help very much here. If a person has been taking amphetamines and really *needs* them, it is common-sense for him to go to a doctor and not to the 'black market'. It's cheaper for one thing, and the doctor knows the correct dosage, and which drugs are most effective. Remember that 'blues' and 'black bombers' *do* have a purpose, and the firms who make them do so in order to help people. A good doctor will understand what dependence on drugs means and will probably prescribe a certain dosage while at the same time 'cutting down' and trying to help the patient to see the emotional causes of his need for them. By treating drug-taking like any other illness we learn not to panic. A wise doctor realizes that while drug-taking, even of the so-called 'soft' drugs, can be very serious, panicking about it does not help at all.

'The Addicted Society'

It is really not individuals who need treatment for drug addiction, but the whole of society. In a sense we are an 'addicted society'. We do rely a great deal on drugs of all kinds – sedatives, tranquillizers, alcohol, tobacco, coffee. But we *depend* on many other things – radio, TV, electricity, and so on. It is hardly surprising that young people experiment with what are, after all, scientific products just like those mentioned above. But more than this, we live in a society which is getting more and more complicated, and more highly organized. We have learned to accept war and destruction and death as a matter of course. It is very easy in such a society to become 'dehumanized'; and it is against a society like this that many teenagers, quite rightly, rebel. Drugs may become part of the rebellion. The trouble is that, by misusing drugs you don't change society for the better; you change yourself for the worse! But it remains true that it isn't good enough to 'cure' the addict; we need to 'cure' our society, too. We need to remain rebels, and not to accept all the evil and waste and poverty and injustice that we see in the world. This is the way in which we can help to treat the social roots of addiction.

QUESTIONS FOR DISCUSSION

1. Are some drug addicts incurable, and if so, what should be society's attitude to them?
2. Describe hospital methods for treating drug addiction. Do you think this is the right approach?
3. How do you think the methods of treating addicts might differ from those used for alcoholics?
4. What do you think is the best way to help drug addicts outside hospital?
5. If you had to open a clinic for drug-takers, how would you run it?
6. Whom would you go to to discuss drug problems?
7. If you could reform mental hospital addiction units, how would you set about it?
8. Do you think religion can cure addiction, or is it just another form of escape? (Read *The Cross and the Switchblade* by David Wilkerson, and discuss it.)

8

A BALANCED JUDGEMENT ON DRUGS

WE want now to summarize the main points of the preceding chapters, so that the *misuse* of drugs (with which we have been dealing throughout this book) can be seen against the background of the *right use* of drugs. More than anything else, and perhaps in this field more than in any other, we need a sense of proportion. In order to reach a balanced judgement on drugs, we need to see the field as a whole. You would not expect to understand the use of beer and wines if you only studied their use by alcoholics, any more than you would understand the working of the body by studying the case-histories of cripples. This is why a slogan such as 'normal people don't take drugs' (which was actually circulated to schools in one area!) is so silly. Quite apart from the fact that the last thing most of us want to be thought is 'normal', if we are thoughtful we know perfectly well that 'normal' people *do* take drugs – of all kinds.

This is why we devoted the first chapter to showing how drugs play a very important part in medical treatment. The idea that drugs are always a 'problem' is quite wrong: we pointed out that many drugs are wonderful means of healing disease and sickness. But we need to remember that a lot of household requisites which we are using all the time are really drugs, or contain them. Antiseptics and disinfectants, for instance, often contain chlorine and iodine. DDT, which we use to kill flies, is a drug (chlorinated diphenyl ether). Similar drugs are used for bleaching powder, skin irritations, eye infections, and so on. We know, too, how valuable a drug like penicillin can be. And we saw that even those drugs which are often misused, in many cases, have a proper medical use; the amphetamines, for instance, are prescribed for fatigue, depression, and severe headaches. Indeed, a drug very similar to what later became known as 'purple hearts' was given in very large quantities to the British armed forces during the Second World War under the name of 'energy tablets', and probably helped them win the war! Of course, there are some drugs which have no medical use at all, but most of what is called 'drug misuse' is a wrong use of drugs which, in themselves, are quite legitimate.

We went on to show how terms like 'addiction' and 'dependence' need to be used with very great care. It is terribly misleading and wrong to class all drug-takers as 'drug addicts'. As we showed, not all drugs are addictive in the same sense, and there are degrees of addiction. To be addicted to a drug means to be dependent on it both physically and psychologically. We should, therefore, use the term 'drug addict' only about persons who depend upon a drug in this way, both physically and psychologically. Very often, newspapers write 'drug addict' when what they really mean is 'drug-taker'. Addiction, we know, is a *relationship* between the personality of the user and the actual drug which he uses.

But to say that a particular drug is not addictive, that it does not produce a physical dependence, is not necessarily to say that it is harmless. There is no apparent addiction, in the strict sense, in LSD, yet in many ways the uncontrolled use of this drug presents us with one of our biggest problems. Indeed, if LSD becomes more widely used in chemical warfare, as it is alleged to have been used in recent years, the consequences for countries as well as individuals could be very serious. Again, as we saw, cannabis is not addictive, but it is certainly possible to become psychologically dependent on it. Because the term 'addiction' has been used so loosely, many people now seem to think that they have only to show that a drug is not addictive to justify the use of it. This is to exchange one over-simplified approach for another, and whatever we think about drug problems, they are certainly not simple!

In chapter 3 we described some of the so-called 'soft' drugs which are commonly misused in this country, and we went on in chapter 4 to discuss heroin addiction. In both chapters we tried to avoid over-stressing the horror aspect of the drugs. There is, in some circles, a strange delight in describing the horror side of drug-taking. Not only is the hysterical attitude a bad way of trying to stop people doing anything (it often has the opposite effect to the one intended), but it is also not an accurate way of seeing the problem. Exaggeration and sensationalism are not the right ways to approach serious questions. If you exaggerate and overstate your case, you only make the truth more difficult to see. And if you shout and scream long enough, eventually nobody will listen to you.

We want to help you to *understand* addiction and what it can mean, and not just get worried or angry about it. And to understand addiction and drug-taking in general, we need to see much more than a merely medical problem. This is why we have (in chapters 5, 6 and 7) discussed some of the psychological problems which may find outlets in drug-taking or may assume other forms. You may have felt that chapters 5 and 6 were hardly about drugs at all! But this was deliberate. What we stressed there was that it is not possible to separate drugs from the kind of society in which they are used, and the kind of problems we face in this society. *Drugs perform a social function.* What are called 'drug problems' are often only symptoms of far deeper and more complex *human* problems.

One conviction has all the time been behind the writing of this book; that telling the truth is the best way to begin to solve problems. We have tried to be honest and to state facts honestly. Some people believe that young people can't be trusted with facts, and that the truth about many subjects should not be told. We do not subscribe to this view. *Truth sets men free and is the best form of inoculation against danger.* It is better to speak the truth and risk the consequences than to hide the truth; for that only leads to deceit, dishonesty and error. This is why we have tried to make this book as full and as accurate as possible. The view that the way to solve a serious problem is to stop talking about it is all too common; it is none the less ridiculous. Problems are solved, not by running away from them and pretending they don t exist, but by facing them honestly and openly, and learning how to handle them.

There are, of course, some risks in speaking the truth. For instance, some people may have known nothing about drugs until they read this book, and, as a result of reading it, they may decide to experiment. We believe that this is a risk which needs to be taken. The alternative is much more dangerous, for far more people come to harm, in the drug field as much as in any other, through sheer ignorance of the facts. Knowledge is the best inoculation against danger. Ignorance on the other hand leads to fear, and can end in disaster.

But one part of truth is what we call *balance*. Balance is necessary because without it only one side of a question is seen, only certain selected facts are given, while others are ignored; and the effect of this can be as dangerous as outright lies. A partial version of the truth is often even more harmful than untruth, and when only some facts are given and others left, the result is not truth but propaganda. There is too much propaganda about drugs, both for and against, which is not based on a balanced and honest desire for the truth. As students, we should always try to be as truthful and as balanced as possible.

For example, on the subject of marijuana, it is dishonest and irresponsible to say, on the one hand, that the drug is terribly dangerous, leading to sexual promiscuity, insanity and death, or, on the other, that its use is always harmless, beneficial and to be encouraged. The campaigners both for and against 'pot' do seem, in many cases, to be incapable of objective study of the evidence. Truth suffers because the protagonists are mainly concerned to defend their respective positions. History shows that one extreme position often gives way to its opposite. Thus, people who start by believing that black (or white) people can do no wrong often end up by believing that they can do no right. Those who start with an over-idealized picture of human nature often end up bitter, cynical and disillusioned; from believing that human beings are easily improved, they have come to believe that they cannot be improved at all. In the sphere of drugs, the attack on marijuana has given way to a romantic attitude which is just as irrational. We need to beware of the propaganda mentality. We need to beware, too, of being slaves to fashion in opinions. To be anti 'pot' is square. That does not mean it is right; nor does it mean that it is wrong. To be pro 'pot' is 'with it' and 'groovy'. That does not mean that it is right or wrong either. The case must be decided on its merits by a balanced approach to the truth. Truth matters more than our prejudices, more than the latest trend, more than all else.

Balance is important in all subjects. In writing a history essay, for instance, you need to be able to see a situation *objectively* in order to discuss its significance. To be objective does not mean to be impartial: but in order for your opinions to be of value, they need to be based on a balanced view of the facts. Balance is necessary in all academic work, and especially in the experimental sciences. But, most of all, it is necessary in those fields where the emotions are easily aroused, and where our judgements may easily be swayed by prejudice. It is easy to become hysterical about subjects of great urgency, like war, race, sex and drugs, and so on. But it is on these subjects above all that a balanced judgement is so much needed.

Let us repeat that to have such a balanced judgement does *not* mean that you are *impartial*. It is not only impossible to be impartial on questions like war and racial hatred; it would be wrong to be. We need to take sides and to stand firm for our principles. But in order to do this, we need to have an informed conscience. Drug-taking is often discussed by well-meaning people of the older generation who see a great evil to be remedied, but who lack balance, and because of this can do a great deal of harm. No great movement in the world ever started without a solid basis of accurate knowledge and deep thought. Movements built on anger, frenzy and panic wither away into fanaticism. So in order to be effective, we need to be informed.

Drug-taking, as opposed to drug misuse, is part of modern society and must be accepted. The use of drugs is a gift of God, but, like all other scientific products, drugs can be misused. Nuclear power can be used for the benefit of mankind or for evil purposes. Drugs can be used to bring health and happiness to men, or they can bring disease, misery and death. But the misuse of something does not damn it altogether. It would be as wrong to deplore the splitting of the atom because men have used its powers for destruction as it would be to condemn all alcohol because it can lead to drunkenness. We need to beware of fanatics in all fields. In discussing drugs, then, we need to remember that it is the *misuse* of them which causes so much pain.

Remember, too, that it is not the drugs themselves which are the *cause* of the pain and unhappiness, but the effects of the drug combined with the problems of the individual and of society. So to 'cure' drug problems we need to look beyond them to the kind of persons we want to be, and to the kind of society we believe in. We need to become rebels against injustice, hatred, self-interest, and all the evils which go to make human life miserable; and to become crusaders for a better world; a world of freedom, peace and love – a world in which we can develop our personalities to the full without relying on harmful drugs. This way lies human progress and the social good.

It may be wondered why we have not mentioned Christianity at all in this book. The reason for this is that it is an easy temptation to offer religion as a slick solution to drug problems. Some would even offer conversion as an alternative to, and cure for, drug misuse. But here, too, we need a sense of balance. It is too easy to exchange one kind of escape for another. You can misuse religion just as you misuse drugs. So we don't offer you Christianity as 'the only answer to the drug problem'. Rather than trying to go on escaping, we want you to face the need to escape.

People want to escape because they are lonely. At its root the whole 'drug problem' comes down to loneliness. We are unable to communicate, unable to find ourselves in the world, and we feel cut off from God and men. One of the most hopeful signs for the future is that many young people since the drug explosion of the 1960s have turned away from chemicals for the solution of human problems. There has been a growing realization that drugs are not the real problem: life is the real problem. So there has started to develop a new search for meaning, for idealism in politics, for spiritual awareness, for true humanity. If we can start to tackle these problems, the problems of drugs will begin to fall into place or subside. Drugs are like the tip of an iceberg . . . the one third showing above the surface, while the dangerous two thirds is lurking below.

GLOSSARY

The following are slang terms used in connection with drugs and drug-taking. Most of the words are in use in the United Kingdom; some are, as yet, only used in the United States. An attempt at definition has been made, but it must be noted that the meaning of some of these terms changes very rapidly and also varies from area to area.

Acid	*LSD*
Acid Head	*LSD taker*
Amp	*ampoule, a container of dangerous drugs, usually Physeptone*
Bad Scene	*Uncomfortable or hostile surroundings, a bad situation, bad vibrations*
Bang	*Narcotic injection*
Barbs	*Barbiturates*
Benny(ie)	*Benzedrine tablet*
Big D	*LSD*
Bird – doing bird	*Serving a prison sentence (rather out-of-date). See also: Porridge, Time*
Black Bomber	*Durophet (amphetamine) 20 mg capsule*
Black and White	*Durophet (amphetamine) 12.5 mg capsule*
Black and White Minstrel	*Durophet (amphetamine) 12.5 mg capsule*
Blocked	*Being under the influence of a drug, alcohol, or both*
To Blow your Mind	*To enter into a frenzied state of mind*
Blue, Bluey	*Drinamyl (amphetamine/barbiturate): but also embracing other pills of the amphetamine type*
Blue Acid	*LSD*
Boy	*Heroin (mostly USA)*
Bread	*Money*
Brought Down	*Depressed state following elated feeling from the effect of drugs*
Bugged	1. *To be irritated by someone or something*
	2. *To be covered by sores and abscesses as a result of neglect from unsterile equipment, etc.*
	(See also: Loused)

Bummer	*Unpleasant experience, especially a bad experience with LSD*
Burn (noun)	*Any substance used for smoking*
(verb)	*To smoke (mainly marijuana)*
Busted	*To be arrested*
Buzz	*Feeling of exhilaration produced by a drug or alcohol.*
C	*Cocaine*
Caps	*Capsules/tablets*
Cat	*Man, sometimes girl*
Charge	*Marijuana*
Charlie	*Cocaine*
Chick	*Girl*
The Chief	*LSD*
Clean	*Off narcotics and/or not carrying drugs at the moment*
Coke	*Cocaine*
Cold Turkey	*Stopping narcotics suddenly without the aid of substitute drugs*
Come Down	*To lose the drug- (or alcohol-) induced exhilaration as it wears off*
Congo Mataby	*African term for marijuana*
Connection	*Person from whom drugs are obtained*
Cook Up	*To prepare an injection by dissolving heroin in a spoon*
	To prepare hashish for inclusion with tobacco, by heating in silver paper.
Crash	*Sleep, pass out from drugs., Also, spend the night in a place (crash-pad).*
Cut	*To adulterate drugs*
Dagga	*South African term for marijuana*
Dealer	*See Connection*
Dexies	*Dexedrine (amphetamine)pills*
Dominoes	*Durophet (amphetamine/sedative) 12.5 mg capsules*
Doobs	*Pills*
To be Down	*To be heavily addicted. Also means depressed*
Dried out	*To have taken a 'cure'*
Drop	*Swallow (a pill)*
Experience	*LSD or mescaline experience*

Fix (noun)	*An injection or a narcotic drug*
(verb)	*To inject a drug*
Flake out	*To lose consciousness (from the misuse of drugs)*
Flash	*Effect of cocaine, and to a lesser extent of methedrine*
	See also: Buzz
Flipped	*To 'go over the edge'*
	See also: Blow your mind
Flushing	*Drawing blood back into the syringe during an injection*
Freak	*A non-conformist, long-hair, drug user. A vague term*
Freak Out	*Psychedelic happening or event*
French Blue	*Amphetamine/Barbiturate pill*
Fuzz	*Police*
Gage	*Marijuana*
Ganga	*West Indian name for marijuana*
Gear	*Belongings, including supplies of drugs, syringes, etc.*
Girl	*Cocaine (mostly USA)*
Goof (verb)	*1. To give oneself up to the Police*
	2. To spoil an injection of a narcotic, either when making it up or when injecting it
Goofballs	*Barbiturates*
Grass	*Marijuana*
Groovy	*Up-to-date with the current trend. Also means beautiful, good, great*
H	*Heroin*
H and C	*Hot and Cold, heroin and cocaine*
Habit	*Addiction to drugs or physical dependence*
Happening	*An event and 'show'*
Hard Stuff	*Opiates and cocaine*
Hash	*Hashish*
Hassle	*An inconvenience, nuisance, bother*
The Hawk	*LSD (mainly USA)*
Head	*Regular user of cannabis or LSD*
Heavy	*Important, serious (a heavy scene)*
Hemp	*Cannabis*
High (adj.)	*Feeling good, in a state of euphoria*
(noun)	*Euphoric state after injection of narcotics*

Hippies	*Persons believing in a way of life based on love and beauty and considering it possible to gain deep insights into life and themselves through the use of marijuana and the hallucinogenic drugs. Also applied to any young person with an interest in psychedelic clothes, music, etc. (Derived from Haight Independent Proprietors, a San Francisco shop in 1966)*
Hooked	*Addicted to narcotics*
Horrors	*Terrifying dreams and hallucinations caused by taking drugs, particularly amphetamine and cocaine*
Horse	*Heroin*
Hung Up	*Unable to obtain drugs; depressed, let down, frustrated, disappointed*
Hypo	*Addict to narcotics* *See also: junkie*
Indian Hemp	*Inaccurate term used by Press, courts, etc. to describe all forms of cannabis*
Instant Zen	*LSD*
Jack	*A heroin tablet*
Jack up	*Take an injection of a narcotic*
Jelly Babies	*Amphetamine-type pills*
Joint	*Cannabis-type cigarette*
Jolly Beans	*Amphetamine-type pills*
Joy popping	*Taking heroin, occasionally mainly sub-cutaneously* *Also taking LSD occasionally* *See also: Skin popping*
Joystick	*Marijuana-type cigarette*
Junk	*Heroin or narcotic drug*
Junkie	*Person addicted to heroin or narcotics*
Kick	*Thrill*
To Kick a Habit	*Stop taking narcotic drugs*
Kief	*North African marijuana*
Loaded	*Full of drugs (or money)*
Loused	*See Bugged (2)*

M	*Morphine*
Machine	*Syringe*
Main liner	*Person who is injecting narcotics intra-venously*
Main lining	*Injecting narcotics intravenously*
The Man	*Policeman or person symbolizing authority*
Mary Jane	*Marijuana (mainly USA)*
Meth	*Methylamphetamine (Methedrine)*
Mike	*A microgramme (of LSD)*
Minstrel	*Durophet: See Black and White Minstrel*
Mud	*Crude Opium: sometimes used for marijuana*
Nicked	*Arrested*
Nigger Minstrel	*Durophet: See Black and White Minstrel*
Nod	*Drowsy state following injection of a narcotic*
O	*Opium*
Out of Your Mind	*See Blocked*
Pad	*Room or flat*
Pellet	*Tablet*
Phy	*Physeptane (Methadone)*
Pill Head	*Person taking pills, usually of the amphetamine type*
Point	*Needle of syringe*
Pop	*Inject*
Popping	*Subcutaneous injection of a drug See also: Skin Popping*
Porridge	*Prison term*
Pot	*Marijuana*
Pothead	*Marijuana user*
Purple Heart	*Out-of-date term, still used by news-papers, etc., for Drinamyl pills (amphet-amine/barbiturate)*
Pusher	*A peddler of drugs*
Reefer	*Marijuana cigarette (not a term used by users, but often by the Press and courts)*
On the Road	*Nomadic life*
Rolling Up	*Making a marijuana cigarette*

Salt	*Powdered heroin (mainly used in USA)*
Scene (the Scene)	*Group of users of drugs, Also used generally to describe a particular group of people*
Score (verb)	*To obtain drugs. Sometimes getting heroin over one's requirements*
Scratching	*Searching for drugs*
Scrip(t)	*Prescription for drugs*
Shit	*Heroin. Also used of cannabis and other drugs*
Shot	*Injection of narcotics. See also: Fix*
Shmee or Shmeck	*Heroin (mainly USA)*
Shrink	*Psychiatrist*
Shoot Up	*Inject intravenously*
Sick	*Refers to opiate withdrawal symptoms*
Skin Popping	*Giving subcutaneous injection of drug See also: Popping, joy Popping*
Skippering	*Travelling about with all one's belongings, sleeping rough. Bedding down with others.*
Sleep Rough	*Sleep anywhere*
Sleepers	*Barbiturates*
Smoke (or to smoke)	*Marijuana or hashish cigarette*
Snort	*Take drugs nasally by sniffing*
Snow	*Cocaine*
Solid	*Marijuana and tobacco cigarette*
Spaced Out	*Out of touch with reality*
Spade	*Negro*
Speed	*Methylamphetamine*
Speedball	*Combination of cocaine with heroin or other opiates (mainly USA)*
Spike	*Needle*
Spliff	*Marijuana cigarette*
Stick	*Marijuana cigarette*
Stoned Stoned out of Your Mind	*Being under the influence of marijuana*
Straight	*Ordinary tobacco cigarette without marijuana*
Stuff	*Heroin or narcotics*
Sugar	*LSD*
Sugar Lump	*LSD*
Sweets	*Amphetamine-type pills*

Taste	*Taking a small amount of a drug and only just feeling it*
Tea	*Marijuana*
Tea Head	*Use of marijuana*
Tie up	*Tourniquet used to prepare vein for injection of drugs*
Time (doing time)	*Prison sentence: serving a prison sentence See also: Bird, Porridge*
Tom (Tom Mix)	*Fix: An injection of a narcotic*
Trip	*Taking LSD*
Turkey	*See Cold Turkey*
Turn On	1. *To smoke a marijuana cigarette* 2. *To give a non-addict his first shot*
Uptight	*Worried, angry*
User	*Taker of drugs, narcotic mainly*
Weed	*Cannabis. Used in dock areas*
Weed Heads	*Marijuana smokers*
White Drugs	*Cocaine. Term not used by addicts*
White Stuff	*Morphine and heroin*
Works	*Syringe, spoon, etc.*
Yellows	*Nembutal*
Zen	*LSD*
25	*LSD* (25) *Lysergic acid diethylamide*

BIBLIOGRAPHY
(*Mainly for teachers*)

These notes for further reading follow fairly closely the headings of the chapters, although obviously there are a number of books which cover more general ground than the specific aspect under which we have included them. There are unfortunately few popular general works on the whole field of drug misuse; some of these we have listed below. Much of the most valuable information is contained in articles in journals. There is an excellent library on the whole field of drug abuse at the Institute for the Study of Drug Dependence, 3, Blackburn Road, London N.W.6 (01-328-5541).

Chapter One. What are Drugs?

Helmuth M. Böltcher, *Miracle Drugs, A History of Antibiotics* (Heinemann, 1963).

Harold Burn, *Drugs, Medicines and Man* (Unwin University Books, 1963).

J. D. P. Graham, *Pharmacology for Medical Students* (Oxford University Press, 1966).

B. Holmstedt and G. Liljestrand, *Readings in Pharmacology* (Pergamon (1963).

Norman Imlah, *Drugs in Modern Society* (Geoffrey Chapman, 1970).

Brian Inglis, *Drugs, Doctors and Disease* (Mayflower-Dell, 1965).

C. R. B. Joyce, 'Drugs and Personality' in B. M. Foss, *New Horizons in Psychology* (Penguin, 1966) 271–284.

C. R. B. Joyce (ed.), *Psychopharmacology: Dimensions and Perspectives* (Tavistock, 1968).

Richard R. Lingeman, *Drugs from A to Z: A Dictionary* (New York, McGraw-Hill, 1969).

J. R. Trounce, *Pharmacology for Nurses* (J. & A. Churchill Ltd., 1967).

Drug use and misuse
Popular general works

Alan Bestic, *Turn Me On Man* (Tandem, 1966). A popular account by a journalist of 'the drug problem' in Britain.

George Birdwood, *The Willing Victim, A Parents Guide to Drug Abuse* (Secker and Warburg, 1969).

Christian Education Movement, *Probe No.* 2, June 1967 (from Annandale, North End Road, NW11). General account intended for schools.

Caroline Coon and Rufus Harris, *The Release Report on Drug Offenders and the Law* (Sphere Books, 1969).

Frank Dawtry (ed.), *Social Problems of Drug Abuse, A Guide for Social Workers* (Butterworth, 1968).

M. M. Glatt, D. J. Pittman, D. G. Gillespie and D. R. Mills, *The Drugs Scene in Great Britain* (Edward Arnold, 1967).

Peter Laurie, *Drugs: Medical, Psychological and Social Facts* (Penguin, 1967).

Donald Louria, *Nightmare Drugs* (Pocket Books, New York, 1966). This small book, only obtainable in the USA, is probably the best introduction to the subject, though the reader should remember that the American terminology differs in some crucial respects from ours.

A. R. K. Mitchell, *Drugs, The Parents' Dilemma* (Royston, Priory Press, 1969).

Martin Silberman, *Aspects of Drug Addiction* (Royal London Prisoners' Aid Society, 1967).

J. H. Willis, *Addicts* (Pitman, 1973).

J. H. Willis, *Drug Dependence, A Study for Nurses and Social Workers* (Faber, 1969).

Frank Wilson, *Miscroscope on Bondage* (Oliphants, 1968).

Anthony J. Wood, *Drug Dependence* (Bristol Council of Social Service, 1967).

More detailed works

Drug Abuse, A Manual for Law Enforcement Officers (Smith, Kline and French Laboratories, Philadelphia, 1966).

Peter Marin and Allan Y. Cohen, *Understanding Drug Use* (Harper and Row, New York, 1971).

The Non-Medical Use of Drugs. Interim Report of the Canadian Government's Commission of Inquiry (Penguin, 1971).

Hannah Steinberg (ed.), *The Scientific Basis of Drug Dependence* (J. and A. Churchill, 1969).

C. W. M. Wilson (ed.), *The Pharmacological and Epidemiological Aspects of Adolescent Drug Dependence* (Pergamon, 1968).

Jock Young, *The Drugtakers* (Paladin, 1971).

Chapter Two. Background to Addiction

Nathan B. Eddy, H. Halbach, H. Isbell and M. H. Seevers, 'Drug dependence: its significance and characteristics', *Bulletin of the World Health Organisation*, 1965, 721–733.

William Sargant, *Battle for the Mind* (Heinemann, 1957).

Chapter Three. The Drug Problem in Britain
Socially acceptable drugs

Henry W. Newman, *Acute Alcoholic Intoxication* (Stanford University Press, California, 1941).

Neil Kessel and Henry Walton, *Alcoholism* (Penguin, 1965).

Sidney Rust, *Smoking and its Effects* (Hutchinson, 1955).

George N. Thompson, *Alcoholism* (Charles C. Thomas, Springfield, Illinois, 1956).

Lincoln Williams, *Alcoholism* (E. &. S. Livingstone, Edinburgh, 1956).

Pep Pills

W. R. Bett, L. H. Howells and A. D. Macdonald, *Amphetamine in Clinical Medicine: Actions and Uses* (E. & S. Livingstone, Edinburgh, 1955).

P. H. Connell, 'Amphetamine Misuse', *British Journal of Addiction*, August 1964, 9–27.

P. H. Connell, *Amphetamine Psychosis*, Maudsley Monograph No. 5 (Chapman and Hall, for Institute of Psychiatry, 1958).

D. Hawks, M. Mitcheson, A. Ogborne and G. Edwards, 'The Abuse of Methylamphetamine', *British Medical Journal*, 21 June, 1969, 715–721.

O. J. Kalant, *The Amphetamines: Toxicity and Addiction* (University of Toronto Press, 1966).

Chauncey Leake, *The Amphetamines* (Blackwell, 1958).

Alan Ogborne, 'The methedrine scene', *New Society*, 26 June, 1969.

P. D. Scott and D. R. C. Willcox, 'Delinquency and the amphetamines', *British Journal of Addiction*, November 1965, 9–27.

Sedatives, Hypnotics and Tranquillizers

Joel Fort, 'The problem of barbiturates in the USA', *Bulletin of Narcotics*, January–March 1964, 17–35.

M. M. Glatt, 'The abuse of barbiturates in the United Kingdom', *Bulletin of Narcotics*, April–June 1962, 19–38.

M. M. Glatt, 'The use and abuse of tranquillizers in alcoholics', *British Journal of Addiction*, January 1959, 111–120.

R. A. Hunter, 'The abuse of barbiturates and other sedative drugs', *British Journal of Addiction*, January 1957, 93–100.

Harris Isbell, 'Abuse of barbiturates', *Bulletin of Narcotics*, April–June 1957, 14.

S. Locket, 'The abuse of the barbiturates', *British Journal of Addiction*, January 1957, 105–107.

Cannabis

George Andrews and Simon Vinkenoog (ed.), *The Book of Grass: an anthology of Indian Hemp* (Peter Owen, 1967).

S. Allentuck and K. M. Bowman, 'The psychiatric aspects of marijuana intoxication', *American Journal of Psychiatry*, 1942, 248–251.

H. Dale Becket, 'Should we legalise pot?', *New Society*, 18 May, 1967.

Ahmed Benabud, 'Psychopathological aspects of the cannabis situation in Morocco', *Bulletin of Narcotics*, October–December 1957, 1–16.

E. R. Bloomquist, *Marijuana* (Beverley Hills, Glencoe Press, 1968).

Cannabis, Report by the Advisory Committee on Drug Dependence (HMSO, 1969).

'Cannabis Sativa' Bibliography, *Bulletin of Narcotics*, January 1951, 59–78, and April 1951, 42–48.

P. A. L. Chapple, 'Cannabis – a toxic and dangerous substance: a study of eighty takers', *British Journal of Addiction*, August 1966, 269–282.

I. C. Chopra and Sir N. R. Chopra, 'The use of the cannabis drugs in India', *Bulletin of Narcotics*, January–March 1957, 4–29.

H. O. J. Collier, 'The essence of pot', *New Scientist*, 31 August 1967.

M. M. Glatt, 'Is it all right to smoke pot?' *British Journal of Addiction*, July 1969, 109–114.

Eric Goode (ed.), *Marijuana* (New York, Atherton Press, 1969).

Lester Grinspoon, *Marijuana Reconsidered* (Harvard 1971).

Indian Hemp (Menley and James, Medical Botany Series No. 6, 1949).

D. McI. Johnson, *The Hallucinogenic Drugs* (Christopher Johnson, 1953).

D. McI. Johnson, *Indian Hemp a social menace* (Christopher Johnson, 1952).

The Marihuana Problem in the City of New York: sociological, medical, psychological and pharmacological studies (Cattell Press, Lancaster, Pa., 1944).

H. B. M. Murphy, 'The cannabis habit', *Bulletin of Narcotics*, January–March 1963, 15–23.

Report of the Indian Hemp Drugs Commission (Government Printing Office, Simla, 7 Volumes, 1893–1894).

John Rosevear, *Pot, A Handbook of Marijuana* (New York, University Books, 1967).

David Solomon (ed.), *The Marihuana Papers* (Bobbs-Merrill, USA, 1966).

Michael Schofield, *The Strange Case of Pot* (Penguin, 1970).

David E. Smith (ed.), *The New Social Drug* (Prentice-Hall, N. J. 1970).

Solomon H. Snyder, *Uses of Marijuana* (Oxford 1972).

Charles Winnick, 'Marihuana use by young people' in Ernest Harms (ed.) *Drug Addiction in Youth* (Pergamon, 1964), 19–35.

P. O. Wolff, *Marihuana in Latin America: the threat it constitutes* (Washington, Institute of Medicine, Linacre Press, 1948).

G. E. W. Wolstenholme and Julie Knight (ed.), *Hashish: its chemistry and pharmacology* (Ciba Foundation Study Group No. 21, J. & A. Churchill, 1965).

LSD

Richard Alpert and Sidney Cohen, *LSD* (New American Library, 1966).

Richard Blum (ed.), *Utopiates* (Tavistock, 1965).

William Braden, *The Private Sea: LSD and the Search for God* (York, Bantam Books, 1968).

Sidney Cohen, *Drugs of Hallucination* (Secker and Warburg, 1965).

A. Y. Cohen, 'Who takes LSD and why?', *New Society*, 11 August, 1966.

R. C. DeBold and R. C. Leaf (ed.), *LSD, Man and Society* (Faber, 1969).

A. Hoffer and H. Osmond, *The Hallucinogens* (New York, Academy Press, 1967).

'Interview with Timothy Leary', *Playboy*, September 1966.

Frank Lake, *Clinical Theology* (Darton, Longman and Todd, 1966) A massive study by a psychiatrist who has used LSD in a clinical context.

Timothy Leary, *The Politics of Ecstasy* (Paladin, 1970).

Timothy Leary, *Psychedelic Prayers from the Tao Te Ching* (League for Spiritual Discovery, P.O. Box 175, Millbrook, New York 12545).

Timothy Leary, R. Metzner, and R. Alpert, *The Psychedelic Experience* (University Books, New York, 1964).

R. E. L. Masters and Jean Houston, *The Varieties of Psychedelic Experience* (Blond, 1967).

David Solomon (ed.), *LSD – the consciousness-expanding drug* (Putnam, New York, 1965).

P. G. Stafford and B. H. Golightly, *LSD, The Problem-Solving Psychedelic* (Tandem, 1967).

R. C. Zachner, *Drugs, Mysticism and Make-Believe* (Collins, 1972).

Drug Traffic

H. J. Anslinger and W. F. Tompkins, *The Traffic in Narcotics* (Funk and Wagnalls, New York, 1953).

Drug Supervisory Body, Geneva, *Estimated World Requirements of Narcotic Drugs* (United Nations, Geneva). (Published annually from 1946 onwards.)

Economic and Social Council, Commission on Narcotic Drugs, *National Laws and Regulations relating to the Control of Narcotic Drugs, Cumulative Index* 1947–1965 (United Nations, New York, 1965), pages 70–72 deal with Great Britain.

Economic and Social Council, Commission on Narcotic Drugs, *Summary of Annual Reports of Governments relating to Opium and other Narcotic Drugs* (United Nations, New York). (Published annually from 1946 onwards.)

Economic and Social Council, Commission on Narcotic Drugs, *Summary of Reports on Illicit Transactions and Seizures received by the Secretary-General* (United Nations, Geneva). (Published monthly.) Volumes XV, No. 12 (1–31 December, 1960) onwards are filed in the United Nations Information Centre, Stratford Place, W1, as are all other UN publications.

International Control of Narcotic Drugs (United Nations, New York, 1965).

Kenneth Leech, 'The East London drug traffic', *Social Work*, April 1966, 23–27.

Norman Lewis, *The Honoured Society: A searching look at the Mafia* (Putnam, New York, 1964).

Permanent Central Narcotics Board (formerly the Permanent Central Opium Board), *Report to the Economic and Social Council on the work of the Board* (United Nations, Geneva, 1947–1961, New York, 1961 onwards). (Published annually.)

Chapter Four. Heroin Addiction (See also under Drug Traffic)

William Burroughs, *Dead Fingers Talk*, Tandem, 1966.

William Burroughs, *Junkie*, New English Library, 1966.

Isidor Chein et alia, *Narcotics, Delinquency and Social Policy: The Road to H* (Tavistock, 1964).

Drug Addiction. Report of the Interdepartmental Committee (HMSO, 1961).

Drug Addiction. Second Report of the Interdepartmental Committee (HMSO, 1965).

D. Gillespie, M. M. Glatt, D. R. Hills and D. J. Pittman, 'Drug dependence and abuse in England', *British Journal of Addiction*, March 1967, 155–170.

M. M. Glatt, 'A review of the Second Report of the Interdepartmental Committee on Drug Addiction', *Bulletin of Narcotics*, April–June 1966, 29–42.

M. M. Glatt, 'Reflections of heroin and cocaine addiction', *The Lancet*, 24 July, 1965, 171.

M. M. Glatt et alia, *The Drug Scene in Britain* (Edward Arnold, 1967).

Ernest Harms (ed.), *Drug Addiction in Youth* (Pergamon, 1964).

John Hewetson and Robert Ollendorf, 'Preliminary Survey of 100 London Heroin and Cocaine Addicts', *British Journal of Addiction*, August 1964, 109–114.

Lawrence Kolb, *Drug Addiction* (Charles C. Thomas, Springfield, Illinois, 1962).

Jeremy Larner and Ralph Tefferteller, *The Addict in the Street* (Penguin, 1966).

Louis Lewin, *Phantastica: narcotic and stimulating drugs, their use and abuse* (Dutton, New York, 1964).

A. R. Lindesmith, *Opiate Addiction* (Principia Press, Bloomington, Indiana, 1947).

Proceedings of the White House Conference on Narcotics and Drug Abuse, September 27–28, 1962 (Washington, Government Printing Office, 1963).

N. H. Rathod, R. de Alarcon and I. G. Thomson, 'Signs of heroin usage detected by drug users and their parents', *The Lancet*, 30 December, 1967, 1411–1414.

Report to the United Nations by Her Majesty's Government of Great Britain and Northern Ireland of the Working of the International Treaties on Narcotic Drugs (Annually, Privately circulated from the Home Office).

E. M. Schur, *Narcotic Addiction in Britain and America* (Tavistock, 1963).

D. R. Wilner and G. G. Kassebaum, *Narcotics* (McGraw-Hill, 1966).

Jim Zacune and Celia Hensman, *Drugs, Alcohol and Tobacco in Britain* (Heinemann, 1971).

Chapter Five. Social Causes of Drug Misuse

These books are not concerned with drug-taking as such, but with the social background, as indeed the chapter itself is.

David Downes, *The Delinquent Solution* (Routledge, 1966).

Christopher Driver, *The Disarmers* (Hodder and Stoughton, 1964).

L. Festinger, S. Schachter and K. Back, *Social Pressure in Informal Groups* (Harper, New York, 1950).

Nat Freedland, *The Occult Explosion* (Michael Joseph, 1972).

T. R. Fyvel, *The Insecure Offenders* (Penguin, 1963).

Charles Hamblett and Jane Deverson, *Generation X* (Tandem, 1964).

Harlem Youth Opportunities Unlimited, *Youth in the Ghetto* (HAR-YOU, New York, 1964).

Bruce Kenrick, *Come Out The Wilderness* (Fontana, 1965). A study of the church in East Harlem.

Lawrence Lipton, *The Holy Barbarians* (New English Library, 1962). An account of the beatnik attitude.

Colin MacInnes, *Absolute Beginners* (Macgibbon and Kee, 1959). A novel of the end of the 'ted' era in London.

J. B. Mays, *The Young Pretenders* (Michael Joseph, 1965).

Richard Neville, *Play Power* (Paladin, 1970).

Jeff Nuttall, *Bomb Culture* (Paladin, 1970).

Mary Morse, *The Unattached* (Penguin, 1965).

John Robinson, *Christian Morals Today* (SCM Press, 1964).

Theodore Roszak, *The Making of a Counter- Culture* (Faber, 1970).

M Sherif, *An outline of social psychology* (Harper, New York, 1948).

Noel Timms, *Bootless in the City* (Bedford Square Press, 1968).

Sally Trench, *Bury Me in My Boots* (Hodder & Stoughton, 1968).

Alex Trocchi, *Cain's Book* (Jupiter Books, 1966).

D. J. West, *The Young Offender* (Penguin, 1967).

L. Yablonsky, *The Violent Gang* (Penguin, 1967).

Chapter Six, Signals and Danger Signs

Social Aid, Church House, Dean's Yard, London, S.W.1. issue a valuable directory called *Drug-Takers, Directory of Aid*, which lists organisations and individuals throughout the country who can be consulted for advice and help.

Chapter Seven, Treatment and Cure for Drug Addiction

Daniel Casriel, *So Fair a House: the story of Synanon* (Prentice-Hall, 1963).

Griffith Edwards, 'The British approach to the treatment of heroin addiction', *The Lancet*, 12 April, 1969, 768–772.

I. M. Frankau and Patricia M. Stanwell, 'The treatment of drug addiction', *The Lancet*, 24 December, 1960.

H. R. George and M. M. Glatt, 'A brief survey of a drug dependency unit in a psychiatric hospital', *British Journal of Addiction*, March 1967, 147–153. On St Bernard's Hospital, Southall.

J. V. Lowry, 'Treatment of the drug addict at the Lexington (Kentucky) Hospital', *Bulletin of Narcotics*, January–March 1958, 9–12.

J. V. Lowry and E. V. Simnell, 'Medicine and law in the treatment of drug addiction', *Bulletin of Narcotics*, July–December 1963, 9–16.

Julius Merry, 'Outpatient treatment of heroin addiction', *The Lancet*, 28 January, 1967, 205–206.

Marie Nyswander, *The Drug Addict as a Patient* (Grune and Stratton, New York, 1956).

Barry Sugarman, 'Daytop Village: a drug-cure co-operative', *New Society*, 13 April, 1967.

'Treatment and rehabilitation of narcotic addicts. Report of the Committee in the Judiciary of the United States Senate', *Bulletin of Narcotics*, July–September 1956, 3–12.

David Wilkerson, *The Cross and the Switchblade* (Oliphants; Hodder and Stoughton, 1967 ed.).

David Wilkerson, *Twelve Angels from Hell* (Oliphants, 1966).

Charles Winnick, 'Maturing out of narcotic addiction', *Bulletin of Narcotics*, January–March, 1962, 1–7.

P. O. Wolff, 'The treatment of drug addicts', *Bulletin of the World Health Organization*, 1945–1946, 455–686.

L. Yablonsky, *The Tunnel Back* (Collier-Macmillan, 1965).

Chapter Eight. A Balanced Judgement on Drugs
Most of the relevant books have been mentioned under earlier headings.

HV
5801
L45   Leech, Kenneth.
1974
        Drugs for young
        people